Himalayan Lust

Himalayan Lust

Sadhguru
Yogi, Mystic and Visionary

JAICO PUBLISHING HOUSE

Ahmedabad Bangalore Bhopal Bhubaneswar Chennai
Delhi Hyderabad Kolkata Lucknow Mumbai

Published by Jaico Publishing House
A-2 Jash Chambers, 7-A Sir Phirozshah Mehta Road
Fort, Mumbai - 400 001
jaicopub@jaicobooks.com
www.jaicobooks.com

To be sold only in India, Bangladesh, Bhutan,
Pakistan, Nepal, Sri Lanka and the Maldives.

HIMALAYAN LUST
ISBN 978-81-8495-076-2

First Jaico Impression: 2010
25th Jaico Impression: 2019

Printed by
SRK Graphics, Delhi

CONTENTS

FACING THE FACELESS

Every year, a group of Isha meditators sets out on a tour of the Himalayas. It is a journey that has been made for centuries by travellers from across the globe. These travellers have found themselves seized by a lust both insistent and primal: a lust for adventure, for an encounter with nature at its most dramatic and awe-inspiring, for a taste of the terrifying stillness at the heart of an epic wilderness. Mountain-climbers, seekers, trekkers, devotees, sadhus, nomads, yogis — all seem to have felt the urge to experience this miracle of soaring earth and plummeting sky.

It is a phenomenon that silences them. It also changes them. On their return, the Himalayas appear to have marked them in some subtle but enduring way. Not surprisingly, the journey has been deemed sacred by diverse spiritual traditions. So in making this annual expedition, the Isha meditators are merely retracing the footsteps of innumerable generations of seekers before them. But there is a difference.

For accompanying them on this trek is Sadhguru – a spiritual master considered by many to be one of the foremost living yogis on the planet. His presence offers the meditators the opportunity to view the entire Himalayan experience through his gaze, and to marvel at his formidable reserves of mystical knowledge and insight.

For those who have known him as an urbane international speaker or as a friendly mentor, the trip invariably comes as something of a shock. For it uncovers a side of him that is unsettlingly remote. A group of Isha meditators on a Himalayan excursion some years ago happened to encounter a woman mystic called Bengali Maa, an intimidating personage, locally revered in the Tapovan region as a saint. When the group mentioned to her that they were on a trip with their guru, she enquired after his antecedents. One of the meditators pulled out a photograph of Sadhguru and handed it to her. She scrutinized it. 'But he is no longer here,' she announced in ringing tones. 'He finished his work and left long ago.'

Stupefied, the meditators reported the incident to Sadhguru. He laughed. 'From the point of view of existence, I no longer exist,' he explained. 'Only life at a certain level of vibrancy, and with karmic appendages, is counted by existence as life. I am off the record as far as existence is concerned. I may have deceived all of you, but here is a woman who could not be deceived.'

Yet another curious incident was the time when a team of
Isha meditators trekking up towards Kedarnath met a group
of around twenty yogis, led by a fierce ascetic, with flowing
hair and smouldering gaze. The leader's air of self-
possession and authority was palpable, and his followers
treated him in a manner that was markedly deferential. When
one of the Isha volunteers mentioned Sadhguru in the
course of a conversation, the ascetic was contemptuous.
'Why are you telling me this? I am not interested. You
obviously cannot see who I am. I am Shiva.'

The statement was unequivocal with no room for argument.
An intense exchange ensued, with the meditator urging the
charismatic yogi to experience Sadhguru firsthand and then
draw his conclusions. But the yogi remained unimpressed.

A short while later, Sadhguru himself approached the scene.
With his hiking boots and sunglasses, he had never looked
less the typical mystic than he did just then. It was then
that a strange thing occurred. The imperious yogi, the self-
proclaimed Shiva, ran up to Sadhguru and prostrated at his
feet.

What did that gesture really signify? What did the ascetic
mean by claiming to be Shiva? And what exactly did he see
that made him bow down so spontaneously at Sadhguru's
feet? Any pat answer runs the risk of ironing out the
mystery, and trivialising the significance of what really
occurred. Perhaps it is sufficient to say that for the

meditators who witnessed it, the experience only confirmed what they already knew — the fact that there is more, much more, to Sadhguru than meets the eye.

This is a book for those who stayed behind. It is a chance to make a pilgrimage on the page, travelling through the unpredictable but fascinating terrain of the master's words. Amalgamating discourses and conversations from several yatras, this book is a blend of the specific and the timeless. Its relaxed, informal mode allows for a spectrum of freewheeling questions, from the quirky to the profound, and for answers that are quintessentially Sadhguru: irreverent, challenging, richly veined with anecdote and legend, and invariably, uncomfortably, bang on target.

This book is not just about the Himalayas. And yet, the book would never have happened without the Himalayas. The mountains play a vital role in the text, alternately as context and catalyst, mood and metaphor. Without them, some of the questions in this book would never have been asked. Even if they sometimes seem tangential to the line of enquiry, they remain a powerful subterranean presence, eventually becoming the very bedrock of this book.

The book allows readers not only to enjoy, but also draw sustenance from Sadhguru's epigrammatic style, his trenchant wit and his gift for telling a good story. Above all, through the conversational rhythms of this text, readers can absorb and revel in the experience of actually being with the master as the adventure unfolded. There are times when they might catch a whiff of wild mountain air, the scent of danger and discovery – perhaps glimpse those landscapes of surreal beauty and spiritual power. And it is possible that they will even catch sight, however fleetingly, of dimensions beyond the geographical – of worlds unknown and undreamt of.

It is a perilous journey, but an exhilarating one. Take a deep breath and begin your ascent.

—Arundhathi Subramaniam

HIMALAYA

Even the rocks reach out to the heavens.
No wonder beings seeking the divine
Made you their abode.

You of gushing waters and rushing air,
Towering presence of unsurpassable grace,

The brave hands that crafted these paths
Into your ceaseless folds —
A mighty effort, but miniscule.

Many have traveled this labyrinth
That seemingly leads to your very womb,

The womb that the courageous ones sought
To die and be born once again.

These Dwijas — the twice born
Of immeasurable wisdom
Left imprints that even
The final deluge cannot erase.

O deathless ones, your energies and wisdom
Live here through me.
I have the keys to your grace and boundlessness

Every beating heart claims to seek.
As I peel to reveal,
The weak-hearted ones run
To save their frailties,

But a few lusty ones remain.
Lust — lust for life — deeper life
Is the only way to unravel
The bounty of nothingness
That is me and you.

—Sadhguru

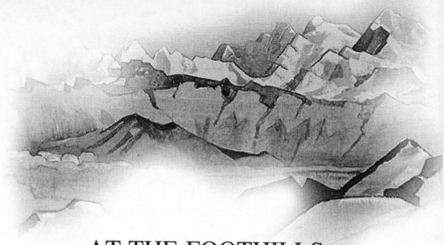

AT THE FOOTHILLS

SADHGURU ON THE SIGNIFICANCE OF THE HIMALAYAS...

'If one is striving to grow, earthquakes and landslides keep happening in one's life.'

The moment you step onto the foothills of Himalayas, a certain romance has begun between the youngest species in the planet, which is you, and the youngest mountain range in the planet — the Himalayas.

Both are still growing, still struggling, still evolving, and still wanting to touch their peaks. But touching the peaks doesn't come easy for the Himalayas. Every day in its effort to grow, it dismantles itself, thus leading to a huge number of landslides and avalanches.

All this seeming chaos is because the mountain range is

making an effort to grow and reach its peak, which is not any different from human life. It's very symbolic. Lots of earthquakes and landslides and disturbances keep happening on a daily basis simply because the mountain is growing. The same is true with human life: if one is striving to grow, earthquakes and landslides keep happening in one's life.

Those who are stagnant, who don't grow, their life seems to be stable and steady, and looks better. But it's lifeless. For one who is striving to grow, an enormous amount of upheaval happens in his life. But all the upheavals are worth a little bit of growth that could happen within a human being.

Now, the first crash happened in the Himalayas some fifty million years ago, and slowly it's been rising at the rate of five millimeters per year. Though the horizontal movement of the continent is about five centimeters per year, the vertical rise is only about five millimeters per year. This is always so with life. If you put in so much of horizontal activity, just a little bit of vertical movement will happen. (Laughs) This is true if you are seeking material well-being, and especially spiritual well-being. If you put in an enormous amount of horizontal activity, just a little bit of vertical movement will happen. That is so for the Himalayas and it is so for you. So the Himalayas and you are very deeply connected; your struggles and the mountains' struggles are very much connected. That's why we let you struggle for these two to three weeks.

It takes enormous intelligence for a person to grow without struggle. Not that it is impossible. Most of the people – in my experience, 99.9% of the people – struggle to grow. Either it takes enormous intelligence, or it takes enormous trust. These are the only two ways one can grow without struggle. Otherwise, struggle is inevitable. Huge volumes of this mountain collapse around itself simply because it is striving to grow. If it becomes stagnant, these earthquakes and these landslides will not happen. But it wants to grow even at the cost of its own well-being. And it can only happen that way for most people.

I have always loved the mountains. Trekking and climbing have always come naturally to me. The Himalayas, these magnificent mountains, have fascinated me since my childhood. Many pictures and books came my way to fuel my urge to trek these vast tracts. Though these mountains have inspired religious hopes and spiritual aspirations in many, I have never looked at them in that way.

One reason why I keep coming back to the Himalayas is that this is one place where there are many who recognize who I am. So I feel at home. Anywhere else I go, I have to play myself down in a way that makes people comfortable. (*Laughs*) This is one place where people can understand life without pretence; people can understand life just as life – not as culture, not as morality, not as ethics, not as religion. They know life just as life, raw life, the way it is. I am very much at home in a place like this.

These mountains are alive with spiritual vibrations. Many spiritual masters have chosen these mountains as their abodes and illuminated the place with their energies. That makes these mountains an inspiring experience for all spiritual seekers. Before you are too weak or old you must meet and merge with these mountains. This is my wish and my blessing.

...AND ON THE SIGNIFICANCE OF LUST.

'Lust is a longing without solution.'

What we are referring to as a spiritual process is basically a journey from creation to Creator. The greediest people on the planet are the spiritual people. All the others are willing to settle for a piece of creation. These people want the Creator himself.

(*Laughs*) A few years ago, a very typically 'spiritual' group of people asked me, 'What is needed, Sadhguru, to grow on the spiritual path?' I said, 'You need lust.' You really need lust, lust for life and deeper life. If that's not there, you cannot grow. They felt extremely offended, because lust and spirituality don't go together. But without lust there will be no spirituality.

What you call 'lust' is a longing for which you have no solution, isn't it? If it is just a desire, there is a way to avert it. If it is just curiosity, there is a way to satisfy it. Lust cannot be satisfied with anything else except finding the goal. Lust is a longing without solution. You must become one with it, or there is no answer for it. So without lust there is no spirituality. The problem is when you say 'lust', people are thinking only of the lust of the body. They are not recognizing the deeper lust that exists in a human being which is far bigger than anything else.

Lust is a compulsive longing. It's inborn. Because it's inborn, it's such a strong and powerful influence. Spiritual lust is also inborn, but because of excessive teaching, people think it's coming from outside. As the longings of the body, the longings of the being are constantly in play. Every human being is naturally spiritual. You are just a spiritual being dabbling with the material, though you think it's the reverse.

There are two aspects to human nature. There is a simultaneous need in every human being for containment and expansion, for self-preservation and boundlessness. Physical nature is trying to protect itself, while spiritual nature is trying to expand. Only the body needs protection. Beyond that, the impulse to preserve is imprisonment. Not understanding these two dimensions, people have divided these two longings in human beings. So they seem conflicting. But in reality, they aren't. You have to maintain the integrity of the boundaries of your body, but beyond that there will always remain something within you that dislikes boundaries.

Do you empower your limitations or your longing to become free? That is the question. Do you walk with your eyes closed or open? That is the question. Are you spiritual consciously or unconsciously? That is the question.

Part One

The Domain of Shiva
Kedarnath

'There are only two or three things in the world which actually overwhelm me — Kedar is one of them.'

For the pilgrim, this remote Himalayan town, flanked by breathtaking snow-capped mountains, located in the Indian state of Uttarakhand, is a site of immeasurable sacredness and antiquity. For the mystic, it is 'the craziest cocktail of spirituality'.

In a spellbinding chapter, rich in metaphor and fable, Sadhguru speaks of the Himalayas as he sees them. He speaks of the variety of yogis who have bequeathed their energies to this distant mountain and left behind the essence of their spiritual discovery for future generations of seekers. It is this bequest — invisible but still vibrantly alive — that makes Kedarnath a living benediction to anyone on the path to self-realisation.

It is impossible to speak of Kedar without speaking of Shiva. The town is the locus of one of the most revered Shiva temples in the country, making it one of the four major sites in India's centuries-old Char Dham pilgrimage. Sadhguru deepens our understanding of this mysterious protagonist who looms large in the spiritual heritage of this land. Invoking him with a strange mix of intimacy and impersonality, he brings Shiva alive in a tantalising variety of ways — as 'emptiness', as 'that which is not', as 'the freedom of the uncreated'; as 'the first yogi and the first guru'; and as fellow-conspirator, as an enigmatic 'fifty per cent partner'.

Sadhguru also speaks of that esoteric dimension of mantras and yantras — the deep connection between sound and form. In the process, he throws light on questions shared by pilgrims and seekers since time immemorial, questions about gods and idols, yogis and adepts, saints and gurus.

Subtle and intriguing, this chapter does not promise to solve any riddles; it only deepens the mystery.

'THIS IS THE CRAZIEST COCKTAIL OF SPIRITUA-LITY ANYWHERE IN THE WORLD.'

The reason we make this trip to Kedar is that this is a place which has witnessed thousands and thousands of yogis, mystics — every kind that you can ever think of — for thousands of years. These are people who made no attempt to teach anything to anybody. So their way of making an offering to the world was by leaving their energies, their path, their work, everything, in a certain way in these spaces. This is the craziest cocktail of spirituality anywhere in the world. No single place has seen this many different varieties of people — people of every kind. When I say every kind, you cannot imagine those kinds.

This activity has been going on in this valley for approximately anywhere between twenty-five and fifty thousand years. The legend goes that this is the place where all the sages and saints lived. That's not just a legend; it's a historical fact. Beyond this mountain is a place called Kanti Sarovar. The legend says that Shiva and Parvati lived there, and they visited Kedar once in a while. It's on the banks of this lake that Ganapati, or Ganesha, was created. It's on the banks of this lake about ten years ago, in 1994 in the month of April, when I came here, that the whole experience of 'Nada Brahma'* happened. Today after ten years we have had the opportunity to go there. It is very difficult to describe the place and what it is.

* This incident, in which Sadhguru experienced all of existence as sound, is described at length in Part Three of this book.

In ancient times, India did not exist as one country, but still it was considered as one entity which was called Bharat Varsha. Its people were not of the same religion, race or language; they did not worship the same gods nor were they politically one. But still the land south of the Himalayas was referred to as Bharat Varsha. So somewhere, there was some sense of unity, because of the common spiritual ethos they carried in them.

Spiritual ethos means, no matter what you are doing, whether you are a king or a peasant, whatever is the nature of your activity, there is only one ultimate goal for everybody – liberation. Even today, even the simplest farmer in this country will talk about mukti. This is a result of the phenomenal amount of spiritual work done in this country. One person who is largely responsible for this, who is of paramount significance in shaping the human consciousness, is Shiva.

In the yogic culture, Shiva is not known as a god, but as the first guru or the Adi Guru. He is the Adi Yogi or the first yogi. Out of his realization, he became ecstatic and danced all over the mountains or sat absolutely still. He was constantly into bouts of stillness and bouts of mad dancing. All the gods who saw him saw something was happening to him that they themselves did not know. Suddenly, heaven felt like a bad place, because this guy is having such a good time! They felt, 'We are missing out on something.' When they finally got him to teach the method, Shiva expounded various types of yoga depending on the level of preparedness of the person who was sitting in front of him.

The first part of Shiva's teaching was to Parvati, his wife. It was taught in a certain intimacy. In great detail, and in very gentle ways, Shiva expounded the ways of yoga to Devi. The yoga sutras of Shiva are such that almost in every sutra, he refers to her as the 'resplendent one', the 'gracious one', the 'beautiful one'. So this teaching transpired between two people in utmost intimacy. Intimacy should not be understood as sexuality. It means that there is no resistance; that this person is absolutely open to what is being offered.

The second set of yogic teachings was expounded to the Sapta Rishis, or the first seven sages. When we use the word 'yoga', don't think it means twisting your body or holding your breath or anything like that. We are not talking about a particular exercise or a technique. We are talking about the very science of creation and how to take this piece of creation — that is you — to its ultimate possibility.

We are looking at gaining mastery over the fundamental processes of life; the very process of creation and dissolution. It doesn't matter at what level of evolution a person is right now; for him also, there is a way. For every being on the planet there is a certain way. That is the advantage of yoga. This teaching happened on the banks of Kanti Sarovar. This is where the world's first yoga program happened.

'[Shiva] has been my fifty per cent partner in everything that I do, but still he overwhelms me.'

For a person who is seeking some kind of spiritual uplift, Kedar is a boon, whose proportions you cannot imagine. That's how it is, if one is open to this. It's very difficult to explain to you what it means; after all, it's just a mountain, just an outcrop of rock. But it's just what the type of people who lived here have done for these thousands of years, what they have done to the space there, which makes the enormous difference.

Now that we are going up in a large group — as we have for the last few years — we need to understand this. In the programs that we do, a million times over I have been saying the same thing, you know: just be with me, just be with me. But for most people, 'what about the food', 'what about the toilet', 'what's happening here', 'what's happening there' — that's been the focus. The few moments of just being there have made some difference, and in so many ways, that's what has brought you here. I would like to say this once again; you just need to be with this. Without deviating yourself, if you do not know what it means to 'be' with something, at least keeping your senses focused is a good way to start being with something. Now, if you are looking at me does not mean you are being with me, but it's a good way to start. You are not capable of looking away from me and being with me, so a good way to start is with your senses.

This is a place that has been specially prepared for the sound, 'Shiva'. When we utter the word 'Shiva', it is the freedom of the uncreated, the liberation of one who is not created. (*Long pause*) He has been my fifty per cent partner in everything that I do, but still he overwhelms me. (*Laughs*) It is not hundred per cent correct to say this, but we can say that the source of the sound 'Shiva' emanates from this space. It's almost like that.

So it's a tremendous possibility. One way of assisting yourself to be with this is that with every step that you take, you utter 'Shiva'. If you want to have a picnic, it's a beautiful place, a fantastic place. I am not against it. If you wish to do it that way, it's up to you. There are no compulsions about this, but if you wish to know something else here, you must minimize yourself. You must simply make yourself very small and every step that you take, we will go with a certain mantra.

So when we say 'Shiva', it's not about creating one more idol, one more god that we can beg to, ask for more prosperity, and for better things in life. It is not about that. The word 'Shiva' means 'that which is not.' Not that which *is*, but that which is *not*. If you want to put it in logical terms, we have been saying everything begins from nothing and ends with nothing. Everything that's here has evolved itself out of nothingness; now it is here; and again it goes back to nothingness. This is a fact of life. That nothingness is Shiva. What we call 'shoonya' is Shiva. That emptiness

is Shiva. You can call it by any name or form, or if you have
that much awareness, you can look at it as a formless energy.
But that which contains everything, that which is not, is
Shiva.

We have given many names to this energy, many forms also.
One important aspect of Shiva is 'Shambho'. Normally,
Shambho, or that aspect of this root energy, is worshipped
only by people who are on the spiritual path, because the
word 'Shambho' means 'the auspicious one.' The most
auspicious thing that can happen to you is to realize
yourself, is to reach the highest within yourself. We think,
unfortunately, that getting married is auspicious; getting a
promotion is auspicious; building a new house is
auspicious... The most auspicious thing that can happen
to you in your life is that you reach the peak within yourself.
At Isha, the energy of Shambho has been very dominant.
In that form we are able to call him down to us here, very
easily. In that form he seems to respond to us much better
than any other form.

There is a very unfortunate tradition right now which says
you should not keep Shiva in your house. It is right; you
should never keep Shiva in your house; you have to keep
him in your heart. Keeping him in your house is of no use.
If you have the courage, you carry him in your heart.
Locking him up in the pooja room won't work, because you
can't lock him up.

One reason why this has been said is that this energy is towards your dissolution; this energy is for you to reach your highest peak. This energy is not for begging; this energy is not for getting a little more advantage out of life. This energy is only for those people who are seeking to reach the very peak of their consciousness. If you are only concerned about getting a little more advantage out of life, maybe we can create many other smaller deities, smaller aspects of life, but not Mahadeva, not Shambho. If you go to the highest, ultimate power in existence, you must also be going with the petition for the highest possibility. You cannot be going with small things to the big man. So that's why they told you, don't keep him in your house. If you are limiting yourself to small things in life, don't keep Shiva in your house. But if you are seeking the highest, you should.

Shiva has always been referred to as 'Triambaka' because he has a third eye. The third eye is the eye of vision. These two eyes are just the sensory organs; they feed the mind with all kinds of nonsense, because what you see is not the truth. You see this person and you think something about him; you see that person and you think something else about him. But you are not able to see the Shiva in him. These two eyes don't really see the truth. So another eye, an eye of deeper penetration, has to be opened up.

In this country, in this tradition, knowing does not mean reading books; knowing does not mean listening to somebody's talks; knowing does not mean gathering information from here and there. Knowing means opening up a new vision or insight into life. So true knowing means your third eye has to open up. If this eye of vision is not opened, if we are limited to just the sensory eye, then there is no possibility of Shiva.

Any amount of thinking, any amount of philosophizing will not bring clarity into your mind. Only when your inner vision opens up, there's perfect clarity. No situation or nobody in the world can distort this clarity within you. But the logical clarity that you create, anybody can distort it. Difficult situations can completely put it into turmoil.

So for what we call Shiva, for that nothingness or for that energy, we have given a form. The form also has been created in such a way, in the tradition, that you should not be able to digest him. He is not a good man. He has got a snake around his neck which you don't like. He's got a garland of skulls which is unimaginable, most uncivilized. At the same time he has such powerful 'tejas' that you can't stay away from him. There is a helpless attraction and a powerful repulsion. That's how the image has been created because the whole idea is to make you understand that this is not something that you logically perceive. Whatever you call God, or divinity, or Shiva, or whatever you want to call it, is not to be perceived logically. It is to be experienced, but never to be understood logically.

You can't arrive at a conclusion that he is a good man. I don't know if you are aware of these things, but in the Shiva Purana, there are such wild stories about Shiva that you can't believe that this could be a god. So, conveniently, a so-called civilization has eliminated all those indigestible stories about Shiva. But that's where the essence of Shiva is.

There are various stories like this. Let me tell you just one to give you some indigestion. You know, there is a story about how the world was created. They say, first of all, there was a Mother who gave birth to three sons – Brahma, Vishnu and Shiva. The Mother is beginning to age and she is concerned that if she doesn't bear more children, the world will end here with these three children. So she wants to be impregnated. But there is no other man in the world except for her three sons. If she has to choose a man, she has to choose one of her sons.

This is something unthinkable. But she approaches Brahma and says, 'The only way to perpetuate the world is for you and me to be like man and woman.' He says, 'It's impossible; you are my mother; I can never touch you.' Then she comes to Vishnu and asks the same question. She says, 'The only way to perpetuate life is for you to be with me like this.' Vishnu is always known to be very diplomatic; he just smiles and he goes away. Then she comes to Shiva. She asks him the same thing. He indulges her without any hesitation. And that's how the world was perpetuated.

So these kinds of stories are there about Shiva, just to make you see that you cannot perceive him through your mind. He is impossible. He is everything that you don't want; at the same time he is the very root of life. That's how the Shiva Purana has been built. The whole idea is to destroy your logical mind so that you open up to a different dimension of life altogether. So if you have to open up Shiva, or that energy which we call Shiva, this one (*referring to the mind*) is not useful. You have to keep it aside. Only then you can feel it; only then you can experience it.

For me, he is alive; for me he is always with me. I never worship Shiva or anybody. But for me he is alive. Every moment of my life, he is there with me. Everything that I do happens out of this. It is not a question of belief; it is not a question of 'do you like this idol very much', or 'what is your ishta devta'. It is just that his energy is always with me. It is within me; it is outside of me. This is a living experience.

If it has to become like this – that God is not something that you worship, but is something that you call yourself, that which is you – then one significant step you need to take is to destroy the logic which separates everything. That is the basic trick with the logical mind; it sets everything apart. If everything has to merge into one, if everything has to become nothing, or if everything has to become Shiva, this mind has to be dissolved.

'This is a place which has housed so many people who just won't fit into your moral structures.'

As I said earlier, Kedar is a very heady mixture of energies. See, when you think of somebody on the spiritual path, probably you would think of them within a certain kind of framework, in terms of a certain kind of behavior, maybe a certain kind of dress, a certain kind of speech. But this is not a land of that kind of spiritual person. The kind that fits into your ways of understanding *has* been here. But there have been many more here who are utterly wild, whom you can never recognize as spiritual. But these are people who have touched the very peaks of existence.

When we say 'a yogi', we do not mean someone of a certain behavior; we do not mean someone with a certain type of morality or ethics. It is just that he is perfectly in tune with life, so tuned in with life that he can dismantle life and put it back together again. The fundamental life that is you, if you can dismantle that completely and put it back, only then you are a yogi. So this doesn't come with ethics; this doesn't come with morality; this doesn't come with good behavior. (*Laughs*) Those things will earn you merit in society, but those things will not get you anywhere when it comes to existence.

So there have been many such incredible human beings. Some of them, as far as the world was concerned, were utter drunkards, but they were yogis. They were drug addicts, but they were yogis; highly abusive people, but they were yogis. All these things in their lives happened not out of some compulsion within themselves; these things happened because they did these things consciously – very consciously. This is a land which doesn't fit into your morality. This is a place which has housed so many people who just won't fit into your moral structures. There are many (*Laughs*) here who abuse every other path in the world, who abuse every other guru in the world – not out of some inner compulsion. They are doing this because unless you think the path you are walking is the best, you cannot involve yourself a hundred per cent. If you think, 'Yes, I am walking this path, but maybe that path is better', then you are not going to walk this path a hundred per cent. Unless you see your guru is the best guru, you can't involve yourself; you can't give yourself to the process. So it is from this understanding that these people are coming. It is not in ignorance that they are making this kind of life for themselves.

So today they have taught you morals and values that [preach that] you must appreciate all the paths in the world. All that is socially very good; spiritually, not good. Suppose you want water and you start digging a well here. In this whole valley, unless you think this is the best place, you won't go all the way and hit the water. You'll dig ten feet, and if somebody comes and tells you that other place seems to be better, and that you can actually get water at five feet, you will go and dig another hole there. If somebody comes and says, 'That would be a better place', you will go and dig another hole there. And in the end, all that you have is holes. Your life will be full of holes, but you will not find anything. Just to avoid this, they created a certain kind of life, which logically doesn't make sense to lots of people. But the very fact that these people attained and lived gloriously, shows it worked.

'Yoga has innumerable devices, innumerable methods of working towards a still mind.'

This yogic tradition has seen thousands of realized masters. No other tradition in the world, no other spiritual culture in the world has seen this kind of galaxy of realized beings. Many methods, many ways, many systems have been evolved. Each master delivered his teaching in his own way; each master employed his own methods and devices as were suitable for people around him.

Fundamentally, the very process of yoga is to realize who you really are. Many methods have been evolved; many devices have been created; many support systems have been devised to make this happen. Each master has made it happen to people in many strange ways. Because every master expresses himself in his own way, each one of them faces different types of resistance in society. The social norm is such. Society knows one guru, a hundred years ago, was doing something in a certain way. So now another one comes today and starts doing things in a totally different way. Now,

either society has to denounce that man or this man. They
cannot see that there are a number of ways to make the same
thing happen.

This reminds me of a great sage in our tradition whose name
was Ribhu. He was known as Ribhu Maharishi. Ribhu had
a disciple, a wayward disciple, whose name was Nidhaaga.
Ribhu Maharishi had a very special love for this particular
disciple, but this disciple was a little wayward, not as focused
as the others. So naturally, among the disciples there was a
little problem: 'Nidhaaga is so unfocused, but why is the
guru so loving to him, and not to us?' There was a problem
going on. These things always happen because a guru is
somebody who is not looking at you for what you are today;
he is looking at you for what you are capable of tomorrow.
What is the possibility that you carry within you? What you
have done till now is of no importance to him. What you
are today is of some importance to him, but what you can
be tomorrow is of utmost importance to him.

Nidhaaga left Ribhu Maharishi and went away. Ribhu
Maharishi made trips to see his disciple wherever he was.
But Nidhaaga was not too receptive. So Ribhu always went
in disguise just to see his disciple and to bless him, to guide
him.

One day, Ribhu Maharishi dressed himself as a village rustic
and went where Nidhaaga was. A king's procession was
passing by on the street. Nidhaaga was intently watching

the procession. So Ribhu Maharishi, disguised as a rustic, went and stood beside Nidhaaga and asked, 'What are you looking at?'

Nidhaaga looked at him in disdain, thinking to himself, 'Everybody is looking at the procession; this fool doesn't even know what we are looking at.'

He said, 'I'm looking at the king's procession.'

Ribhu Maharishi asked, 'Where is the king?'

'Can't you see? He's sitting on the elephant.'

'Oh, but which one is the king?'

Now Nidhaaga got really angry and he said, 'Can't you see, you fool? The man who is sitting above is the king; the animal below is the elephant.'

'Oh, what is this above and below? I don't understand.'

Now Nidhaaga became really furious. He said, 'You fool, you do not know what is above and below? It looks like what you see and what you hear doesn't seem to get into you. You need some action.'

He bent Ribhu Maharishi forcefully down and stood on his shoulders. 'Now do you see? Now I am above, you are below;

I am the king, you are the animal. Did you get it?'

'Not really! Now I can understand what is man, and what is elephant. Now I can understand what is above what is below. But what is this 'you' and 'me' you are talking about?'

Suddenly the basic questions of 'Who am I? Who are you?' struck Nidhaaga. He fell at Ribhu's feet as he realized that it could not be anybody other than his master, and he attained self-realisation in that moment.

So each master employed his own ways, his own methods to do things. Some were subtle; some created dramatic situations. In Isha (*Laughs*), I don't want to reveal the method, because once you reveal the method, you have to create a whole new method. (*Laughs*) Any method works only when you just walk into it and it happens to you. If it is all told to you, it doesn't work. So here we have our own methods, very subtle. For some we have subtle methods; for some we have dramatic methods; for some we have knocking-on-the-head type of methods. There are various kinds of methods.

Searching for truth is itself a big illusion because whatever we term the truth is always and everywhere. We don't have to search for it; we don't have to seek it; it always is. Now the only problem is your inability to experience life beyond what you call mind; or right now your capability to experience life only through the limited dimension that we call mind. That is the only problem.

Patanjali Maharishi defined yoga as chitta-vritta-nirodha. It means that if you still the modifications, or the activity of the mind, you are there: everything has become one in your consciousness. So yoga has innumerable devices, innumerable methods of working towards a still mind. We may be pursuing many things in our lives; we may be going through the processes that we call achievements in our life. But to go beyond the modifications of the mind is the most fundamental, at the same time the highest achievement, because this releases a human being from what he is seeking, from what is within and what is outside, from everything. He becomes an ultimate possibility if he just stills his mind.

Whatever we may be seeking in our lives, whatever we may be doing in our lives right now, whatever most people are after right now in their lives, is fundamentally to achieve happiness and peace. Most people spend a whole lifetime and never get to be truly happy or peaceful. Now not being happy or not being peaceful are also certain states of the mind, a certain expression of your energy. If you're happy, your energy is expressing itself in a certain way; if you are unhappy, the same energy is expressing itself another way; if you're angry, it is finding a different type of expression; if you are in frustration, another type of expression; in fear, anxiety, another type of expression. It is the same energy finding different types of expression. Definitely, every human being, no matter which path he is pursuing, fundamentally, he is doing whatever he wants to do right now because somewhere he believes that will bring him happiness and peace.

Whatever happiness and peace that one knows in one's life is generally so fragile that it is always subservient to the external situation. So most of your lives go in trying to manage a perfect external situation which is just impossible to do. No human being is ever capable of creating a perfect external situation because the outside situation will never be a hundred per cent in your control, no matter how powerful a human being you are. So yoga focuses on the inner situation. If you can create a perfect inward situation, no matter what the external situation, you can be in perfect bliss and peace.

This reminds me of a certain situation that happened in the South Indian yogic tradition. Once there was a devotee whose name was Tatvaraya. Tatvaraya encountered a very beautiful master in his life; his name was Swaroopananda. This master never spoke. As a human being, he spoke here and there; but as a guru he never spoke. This was a silent master. Tatvaraya found tremendous bliss and joy in being with his guru, and he composed a bharani. The bharani is a certain composition in Tamil, which is generally composed only for great heroes.

So society reacted and protested that a bharani cannot be

composed for a man who has never even opened his mouth, who has not done anything except sit quietly. This can be composed only for great heroes. A hero was generally in the past described as a man who has slain one thousand elephants. You know Veerappan? (*Laughs*) So that's a real hero who can slay one thousand elephants! And this man has never even opened his mouth; he just sat quietly; surely he doesn't deserve a bharani? Then Tatvaraya said, 'No, my master deserves more than this, but this is all I can give.'

So there was a big argument and debate in town about this. Then Tatvaraya decided the only way to settle this issue is to take these people to his master. And he took this group of people into the forest. His guru was sitting quietly under a tree. All of them went and sat there, and Tatvaraya explained the problem: 'People are protesting because I composed a bharani in your honor; it is supposed to be composed only for great heroes.'

The master heard all this and just sat quietly. All of them sat quietly. Hours passed; they sat quietly. A few days passed; they sat quietly. After about eight days of all of them just sitting quietly, Swaroopananda moved his mind. At that point, everybody's thought process became active. Then they realized a true hero is somebody who has tamed these rutting elephants that you call mind and ego. And both these elephants were still for these eight days for everybody by just sitting with the master. And they said, 'Yes, this is the man who truly deserves a bharani.'

'A yogi is somebody who is able to dismantle his own creation and put it back together again.'

Seeker: Sadhguru, you've said that Shambho is a 'form' of Shiva. What exactly does that mean? I'm not sure I understand. I thought you said Shiva was a mantra. And if Shiva is a mantra, how does a mantra have a form? Is Shambho a form of Shiva, a mantra or a state of being?

Sadhguru: See, this culture was created as a science to enable you to seek your ultimate liberation. Every aspect of your life – whether you sing, dance, eat, or study – was only aimed at your mukti. Your religion, education, family, and your business, all these things are secondary; the only thing that matters to you is your mukti. That's how it's supposed to be, isn't it? So when mukti is the only thing that you're seeking, everything is oriented towards that.

Dance was not entertainment. If you get deeply involved in it, you will become meditative. That's how it was structured. Music was not entertainment either: if you get deeply involved in it, you become meditative. Everything was oriented only towards your emancipation, taking you towards ultimate liberation.

This culture has looked at it this way for a long period of time. Over ten thousand years or even more, it did not know any disturbance. A well-settled society, constantly looking at liberation – you know in how many million ways they could have developed people? All because the whole society's intelligence is focused in one direction? Every possible way of exploring your inner nature was brought forth. Nowhere else in the world – you can investigate it as much as you want – have people understood the interiority of a human being as this culture has. With enormous depth, it has been looked at – not the surface, but the very core of the human being. It is just that because they're subjective sciences, they were expressed in certain ways, coded in certain ways, so that logically you cannot misinterpret them. Such care was taken to see that misinterpretations don't happen. In spite of that, over a period of time, misinterpretation invariably happens, and the science needs to be rejuvenated.

So as a part of this, this culture also created various energy forms which could be conducive to your growth. This creation of energy forms – powerful energy forms through which one can seek one's own growth and well-being – is again another dimension of what we call consecration.

The Dhyanalinga*, for example, is an energy form. It took

---

*A powerful energy form with intense vibrational energies, this is the first of its kind to be completed in over 2,000 years. Consecrated by Sadhguru in June 1999, the Dhyanalinga multi-relgious yogic shrine at the Isha Yoga Centre in Coimbatore offers a unique space that induces deep states of meditativeness in all who sit in its presence. It subscribes to no particular faith or belief system, and requires no ritual, prayer or worship.

eighteen or nineteen years of preparation, and about three-and-a-half years of intense consecration. People who witnessed what happened in these three-and-a-half years have never been the same again. Hundreds of people were witness to this. What they saw is so miraculous that if they talk to anybody about it, it will be pure mumbo-jumbo. Nobody will believe that such things can happen. Absolutely incredible things were happening around that whole space during the consecration. This is what we mean by creating an energy form.

You see the stone linga; that is not significant. The stone linga was used only as a scaffolding to create an energy form. Once the energy form was created, actually we could have removed the stone linga. Nothing would change. But people want to see things with their eyes, otherwise they cannot relate to it. And also we spent a lot of money, so we won't remove the stone linga! But actually, as far as your experience and the energy is concerned, even if we remove the stone linga, it will still be the same. Nothing will change there.

Generally, the word 'linga' is referred to as the 'form'. Why we are calling it the 'form' is because today modern cosmologists are telling you the core of every galaxy is a perfect ellipsoid. Are you aware of this? The core of every galaxy is always an ellipsoid. A perfect ellipsoid is what is referred to as a linga. You know what an ellipsoid is? An ellipsoid is a three dimensional ellipse. So the first form — from the unmanifest to manifest — that creation takes, is always the form of an ellipsoid. This is something cosmologists are saying today. And from our experience we know that if you raise your energies to a certain pitch, the final form that your energy takes before dissolution is also that of an ellipsoid. So the first form is the linga; the final form is also the linga. This is why the linga is seen as a doorway to the beyond, from both ends. Because the A and Z of creation happen to be the linga, it is seen as a doorway to the beyond.

So the word, 'Shambho', is associated with this. Is it a mantra? Yes. What does a mantra mean? Now, modern science is telling you that the whole existence is just a vibration. That means the whole of existence is just sound. In this complex arrangement of sounds which you call creation, there are a few key sounds. These key sounds can open up dimensions for you. So that is what is being referred to as a mantra. Every sound is a mantra. But we are referring to certain sounds as mantras, because they are key sounds. If a key is given to you, you could start loving the key, hugging or kissing the key, but it doesn't do anything. If a key is given to you, you just have to understand where you should insert it and how you should turn it. It can open up a whole world for you. So a mantra is a device that you learn to use in a particular way. If you know how to use the particular mantra with the right sense of awareness, it can open up a completely new dimension of life for you. If you were just emotionally attached to the mantra – you know, emotions can be juicy and nice – it won't lead you anywhere.

So what you call as a mantra is basically a device.

Is it a form? Yes, because every sound has a form attached
to it. The word, 'Shambho', has its own form. Is it a person?
Yes. Is it a living thing? Yes, very much, because everything
in the existence is alive. From a single atom, a rock, a tree,
a plant, to an animal, everything is alive actually, isn't it?
Whether you are able to perceive this or not, that's the only
question. Right now, you're breathing; the air is alive, that
is why it can give you life, isn't it? Maybe it is not alive
like you, but it is alive in its own way. Because of this,
here in this culture, we started looking at life in a different
way.

This is a culture which worshipped trees, which worshipped
the earth that you walk on, the water that you drink, the
food that you eat. Generally, everywhere in the world, if food
appears in front of people, they will thank the god that they
have not seen for it. Here, we have no such etiquette
problems. Here we just bow down to the food itself. We
don't know what gods created this. Do you know? You really
don't know what gods created this. All you know is, if you
do not eat this, you'll fall dead. All you know is that this
food on your plate is actually going to become you within
the next few hours, isn't it? This is sustaining your life. So
you become reverential to the food that you eat.

If you eat your food reverentially, whatever you eat will work
miraculously within you. The water that you drink, you

become reverential to it, because over seventy per cent of this body is water. When you value your body, should you not value the ingredients which make this body? You cherish and love your husband, wife, child, mother, father, isn't it? If you love them, then the ingredients that make all these people – should you not be reverential to them? If water plays havoc in your mother's body, she's finished. Yes or no? If air plays havoc in your husband or wife's body, they're finished. If earth, fire, or any aspect of the five elements just go a little out of hand, your husband, wife, child, mother, father are finished. Isn't it so? So, every moment, it is these five elements which are sustaining you, nourishing you, and making things happen. You just become reverential to that. Every aspect of existence actually has something to do with your life, isn't it? If some imbalance happens in some galaxy, you could just evaporate the next moment.

So this tradition created certain powerful forms, well-established forms, that you can call for. In certain systems of yoga, people master these forms. You have heard these kinds of things. Ramakrishna Paramahamsa used to feed Kali with his own hands and she used to eat food. This is a hundred per cent reality, I'm telling you. For any logical, thinking mind, it looks like absolute nonsense, isn't it? It looks like he must be hallucinating. He's not hallucinating. It is just that his consciousness is so crystallized, whatever form he thinks of and reveres, he just creates it right there. So if you want Kali, Kali is right there. Anything that you want can be created right there, simply because all these forms were established long ago for sadhana.

Different yogis, different systems created various forms.
There are very beautiful forms and very hideous forms.
Shambho is one of the more auspicious ones. He is a very
gentle form of Shiva, which is rare. Shiva is usually wild
and crazy. But this is a very gentle form of Shiva, a beautiful
form. These forms were established by people so that others
could make use of it. They are made into eternal forms. If
you are willing, you could bring them down in your
experience. Is this a reality? Is this something that is there
in the creation? No, these things were created by people who
had absolute mastery over their own systems, their own
energies and their own creation.

When we say somebody is a yogi, it does not mean he stands
on his head, or holds his breath. A yogi is somebody who
is able to dismantle his own creation and put it together
again. These are the fundamentals of yoga. The basis of yoga
is in what is called bhoota shuddhi. You know the pancha
bhootas? The five elements in nature? It means having
absolute mastery over the five elements which make you.
So once you have this mastery, you can dismantle yourself,
and put yourself back once again. So that is what yoga
means. Knowing the science of yoga means that you know
every nut and bolt of your creation. You have gone into the
depths of who you are, on all levels: the physical body, the
mental, the energy levels, much deeper levels. You have seen
everything, the way it is within yourself. It is from that

context that you exist because what you call 'myself' is a mini cosmos by itself. If you know this one, you know everything. Everything that is worth knowing in existence you know the moment you know yourself.

'Shiva is constantly waiting for one moment of vulnerability in you when he can crack you.'

Seeker: So does chanting 'Shiva Shambho' help us on our trek up these mountains? And would it be appropriate to continue chanting 'Shambho' afterwards as well?

Sadhguru: When you say 'Shambho', when you say 'Shiva', you are not asking for help. Now if you are saying 'Shambho' every time your knees are hurting, that's not it. (*Laughs*) Shiva bhaktas always called upon Shiva and said, 'Shiva, please destroy me.'

Have you seen that panel about Akka Mahadevi in the Dhyanalinga temple? Akka called upon Shiva and this was her prayer: 'Shiva, when I am very hungry, if I get a morsel of food, before I put it in my mouth, let it slip and fall into the mud. And before I bend down and pick it up, let a dog come and take it away. And if I am climbing a mountain, let my feet slip and let me fall down and let my head break.' This is how the prayer goes. (*Laughs*) Is that how you were calling Shambho? (*Laughter*)

This is a trick. You will see tomorrow early morning when

you go to the Ganga to wash all your sins, particularly if
you go there where its very crowded. You will notice that
it's not so cold right now, yet the water is quite chilled in
the mornings. They're all saying, 'SSShhivaa-shivvaaa!'
When they are having a warm water bath, are they saying
'Shiva, Shiva'? No. (*Laughs*) They are whistling or singing
some film tune. In chilled water, it's 'Shiva, Shiva, Shiva'.
(*Laughs*) This is not about Shiva; this is about your survival.
You're just calling the wrong guy. If you are seeking survival,
you are just calling the wrong person. Shiva is constantly
waiting for one moment of vulnerability in you when he can
crack you, okay? He is not seeing how to help you to survive.
He is just waiting for a moment of vulnerability when he
can squash you. So I asked you to say 'Shambho' with that
intention, not with the intention of helping you up the
mountain.

As I mentioned earlier, out of a very deep state of
understanding of sound, we have taken out a few sounds
which are like the keys to existence. If you utter them with
the right sense of intensity at the right moment in your
life, they can just shatter all your limitations and take you
elsewhere. So 'Shiva' and 'Shambho' are two such keys. You
are supposed to use these to break you open, to crack you
up. From the solid person that you are, they are meant to
open you up to a new dimension. Not 'Shiva, Shiva, Shiva'
to help you to go up the mountain; that is not the way it
was given to you. Just make it your life-breath, to make the
sound constantly on within you. If one moment of

vulnerability comes, the sound will just crack you open. New things will happen; absolutely new things will happen.

So don't use 'Shiva Shambho' for your survival. You say 'Shambho' because you want to dissolve with this sound. Not because you want to become something with this sound, not because you want to buy a condo in Florida, not because (*Laughs*) you want to buy a new house, or you want to buy a new vehicle, or you want to get your daughter married. That's not the reason why you say 'Shiva'. When you say 'Shiva', you are seeking dissolution, because Shiva means 'that which is not'. The blissfulness of the uncreated, the ecstasy of being uncreated, that's what Shiva means. When who you are, is broken, only then you will be ecstatic. If you have known a moment of ecstasy in your life, those moments happened only when who you are was broken for some reason. Isn't that so? When you are yourself, you will never know a taste of ecstasy or blissfulness within you.

Can I continue to say 'Shambho'? If this is your intention, you must always say it. If this is not your intention, if you are just thinking of how to acquire the next property, call on someone else. Don't call on Shambho and Shiva. It will not be appropriate. Not that they cannot provide it, but it'll be like using a spacecraft to go to the next village. You can walk to the next village. If your intention is to go to Mars or beyond, a spacecraft is okay. But don't ride a spacecraft to the next village.

There is a wonderful story in the yogic lore about the kriya yogis, yogis who have mastery over their life energies. Usually if they have attained to their heights, it's fine. But otherwise as they get more and more mastery over the situation around them and they can do things that other people cannot, they tend to have a total disdain for everything else around them. (*Laughs*) So they look down upon all these mantra-uttering people.

One day a kriya yogi, who had great accomplishments behind him, went to Shiva and asked, 'What is all this? Your bhaktas are making all this noise in the world; all the time they are shouting, 'Shiva Shambho'. What is this going to do? What is the use of yelling these mantras like this?'

Then Shiva said, 'Let us experiment. Here is a worm crawling. Go close to him and say, 'Shiva Shambho'. Let's see what happens.'

The yogi went to the worm and said, 'Shiva Shambho'. The worm fell dead.

The yogi was aghast: 'I just uttered this mantra, your name, and the worm is dead! What is this?'

Shiva, completely oblivious of the worm, pointed at a butterfly and said, 'See how wonderful this butterfly is.' The yogi also got involved with the butterfly. Shiva said, 'Attempt the mantra with the butterfly.'

The yogi looked in the direction of the butterfly and said, 'Shiva Shambho'. The butterfly fell dead.

The yogi was totally in turmoil, and said, 'What is this? If I just utter your name, one creature after the other is falling dead. I don't want to say it anymore.'

Shiva completely ignored this and looked at a wonderful deer that was romping around. He said, 'Look at the deer, so wonderful.' The yogi also got involved. Shiva said, 'Why don't you utter the mantra to the deer and see?'

The yogi said, 'Shiva Shambho'. The deer fell dead.

The yogi said, 'No! No more can I say this.'

Then somebody brought their newborn child to Shiva for his blessings. Then Shiva said, 'Why don't you utter the mantra to this child?'

The yogi said, 'No, I cannot do this. (*Laughs*) Already the worm, the butterfly and the deer I have behind me, and I don't want to say this.'

Shiva said, 'It doesn't matter; say it.' So the yogi, with great hesitation, went to the child and said, 'Shiva Shambho'.

This newborn babe just sat up, looked at the yogi and said, 'Oh yogi, don't you know the power of the mantra? Don't you know the power of the name of Lord Shiva?'

The yogi said, 'No, can you tell me?'

The infant said, 'Yes. I was a worm and you uttered the mantra, so I became a butterfly. You uttered the mantra, so I became a deer. You uttered the mantra, so I became human. You utter the mantra once more, I will become divine.'

'You can transform this piece of earth into the divine... a deity that's worthy of worship.'

Seeker: I'm not sure how to ask this question, Sadhguru. You look just like the rest of us, but I know you are not like any one of us. What do you plan to accomplish by playing this game with us? When do you intend to show us your real form?

Sadhguru: She says I look just like her – do you believe this? What she means is that I look like everybody here in flesh and blood, but she thinks or she feels I seem to be something else. So why am I playing this game of being like everybody? When am I going to show my real form?

Whichever way I express myself, I am bound to be misunderstood. So I am just thinking of what would be a constructive misunderstanding. (*Laughs*) I don't expect understanding, so I'm trying to choose a constructive misunderstanding.

See, this body can just be a bundle of flesh and blood and bones, of course. Or this body can be made into a powerful instrument. When you make it into a powerful instrument, with a possibility of access to dimensions of the beyond, then you call this a deity. You know, why so many deities are established everywhere in the country is that people learned the science of establishing a form which will become a means, which will become a gateway, which will become a doorway for experiencing another dimension that is not in your experience right now.

So if you stay in the ashram, you have to do yoga. Bending this body, twisting this body, holding this breath, doing this and that, is just to slowly transform this mass of flesh and blood. See, you transformed mud into a human body. Quite a transformation, isn't it? The food that you eat is just earth, a piece of earth; you transformed it into this pulsating mass of flesh. But you know this mass of flesh only has a certain span. When the span is done, it is going to become a piece of earth once again. So this transformation of a piece of earth into this possibility of being a human body is a tremendous possibility. Either it remains just a possibility or it becomes a force of transformation. A possibility means it is a door – whether somebody walks through the door or not, is always a question.

So this human body has come with a certain possibility.
This body when it's born, generally, has come as a biological
entity. The only forces which work through it are self-
preservation and procreation. This is all it knows. But if you
do a little bit of work with this, you can transform this piece
of earth into the divine itself. You can make it into a deity
that's worthy of worship.

How to make this happen – there is a whole science behind
this. There are so many deities in India; there are over three
hundred thousand gods in India. Now, all these things are
not just a joke; most of them are well-established forms that
one can make use of for one's well-being, growth,
transformation and liberation. Most of the deities were
established for well-being; a few of them were established
for liberation. Always people who are seeking ultimate
liberation have been on the worship of Shiva because Shiva
is the destroyer. So this is a form that has been very well
established as a force to destroy your ignorance and your
limitations. Is he real? As real as you are.

You asked this question – you know you come from a
Veerashaiva* community. All the pujaris in Kedar were
Veerashaivas. Did you know this? Oh, you did not meet

*The Veerashaiva (literally, 'heroic devotees of Shiva') or Lingayat sect is believed
to have been founded by five gurus – Revana, Marula, Ekorama, Panditaradhya and
Vishwaradhya – who sprung from the five heads of Shiva, almost about 5,500 -
6000 years ago. Basavanna, the revered saint, reformer, thinker and teacher of the
twelfth century, is regarded by some as the originator of the faith, and by others as
a significant reviver.

them? They were all your clan. (*Laughs*) They left Karnataka long ago. Veerashaiva means brave or valiant or militant followers of Shiva. If you look at some of the greatest of the Veerashaiva saints, I think the best example would be Alama Mahaprabhu. Alama praises Shiva to glory, worships him, but many times he plays with Shiva like he is a little kid, because at that moment Alama is much larger than Shiva himself. At a certain other moment he is looking up to Shiva and crying; at a certain other moment he plays with Shiva.

People often ask me, what about this Shiva and you? They say, in many ways you are religionless, you are godless, but what about this Shiva? So I usually tell them that Shiva is my fifty per cent partner. Sometimes he is a sleeping partner; I am the active partner. Sometimes I am the sleeping partner; he is the active partner. (*Laughs*) We keep playing this game between the two of us. If both of us work together, then one world will not be enough; we will need two. So we never work together. This arrangement is working very well for me. Now this sounds audacious, but that is the reality.

Maybe people from outside cultures won't understand this fully. But for people who are born in this culture: everything that you think Shiva is, I am. (*Laughs*) That is the reality in many ways.

'It's a privilege that, when you want to give, there is somebody to receive.'

Seeker: When we reached Kedar, I just wanted to sit outside the temple and meditate, but we were encouraged to visit some sadhus. It struck me then that if we have you with us, where is the need to go pay our respects to a sadhu and get prasad from him? I have always felt that sitting and being with you is more than enough. So why go and seek the darshan of someone else?

Sadhguru: Now the very moment you say, 'why should I go to some sadhu', you don't know who I am either. You don't know who he is. He may be just a beggar, or he may be Shiva himself. You don't know. So when you don't know, the best thing is if you see an ant, bow down to it; if you see an elephant, bow down to it; if you see a beggar, bow down to him; if you see a plant, bow down to it. You don't know how to distinguish one thing from the other, isn't it? When this is your condition, the safest thing for you is to bow down to everything.

See, a blind person when he walks, you know what he does? He takes the stick, and taps everything. Whatever it is, he taps and feels it, because when you're blind that's the best way to walk, isn't it? Since you are still blind, so you don't decide what is sacred, what is not sacred. You just bow down to every rock, every animal, every insect, every plant, every human being, everything. Whether he is a sadhu, or a beggar or a prostitute, you bow down to every one of them, because you don't know who is who. You just don't know who is who. So don't say 'some sadhu'. You don't speak like that about people.

Seeker: But still, Sadhguru, seeing these sadhus is very intriguing, and yet very confusing, because it is hard to know who is real and who isn't real. I was trying very hard not to be judgmental, but so many of them come, pull at you, want money — that sort of thing. What is the appropriate way for us to interact with these people?

Sadhguru: Now, this is an endemic problem with people. People always want to know whether they are going to the right place or not. If they water the garden, they want to make sure they are watering only the fruit-bearing trees, not the weeds. If they give money to somebody, they would like to give to somebody who deserves it, not to somebody who doesn't deserve it. So when I am giving the money, is this man really holy, or is he just a beggar? Is he exploiting me? All these questions.

Now, the sun rose in the morning, gave himself totally to the weeds and the flowering trees and the fruit-bearing trees, to the good man and the evil man, to the criminal and the saint, the same way. The little, petty things that you have to give, why do you calculate so much about making a mess out of your life? If you have something to give, you give. Whether that person deserves it or not, that's not your business. If you don't want to give, don't give; that is also okay. It is not that you must be giving all the time. If you have a feeling of giving, you just give. The man may be a thief; that's not your problem. The man may be a great saint; that is also not your problem. You want to give, so you give joyfully.

Why do you calculate? Because you want to know, whatever you're giving, if it's earning you enough good marks. This is very bad karma. It is not necessary for you to keep accounts of what you give. What you feel like giving, joyfully you give; otherwise please don't give anything. Just shut yourself off from people and life around you, and just see what you can do with yourself. That is also all right. But you have a certain emotion in you: you want to give; you don't want to look like a stone; you don't want to be looked upon as a stingy, uncaring person.

Now if a blind man comes and begs, people want to pull his eyelids and see whether he's really blind or not. It's not your business. If a man is willing to dig himself to such a point that he has to pretend to be a blind man just to get a rupee out of you, he deserves the rupee; he's so pitiable. So you don't have to pull his eyelids and see whether he's really blind or not. So for you to give, it is not necessary that somebody should be in a pathetic condition, or somebody should be in a limited condition. The giving is about you, not about the other person. Be glad there is somebody to receive. That's the wonderful thing about India. If you have some extra food, you can call anybody on the street and give it to him. Nowhere else in the world can you do this. It's a privilege that, when you want to give, there is somebody to receive.

Don't you bother about whether somebody is holy or unholy. Especially if somebody is unholy, he needs more giving, isn't it? If somebody's holy, if somebody has reached a certain state, whether you give or you don't give makes no difference to him. But if somebody is in a pathetic condition, he's the one who needs to receive things from you. You joyfully shower it upon him to the extent that you can. There is no compulsion; nor will you go to heaven because you gave. It is just that you have a link to him, so you give. Nobody's keeping accounts of how many rupees you gave on this trip except yourself. It would be good if you also did not keep account. If you feel like giving, give. Otherwise, don't bother about it.

'Once you distance yourself from the physical, you are in complete charge of your life.'

Seeker: We saw some sadhus who weren't wearing any clothes, just walking around naked. How is it possible for them to be like that in such a climate?

Sadhguru: Maybe they were thick-skinned! (*Laughter*) One thing is they are smearing themselves with vibhuti, which is doing something to them. There is a certain kind of sadhana also. Another thing is that they have not made their bodies so important. If you don't make your body important, you can stretch it to all kinds of limits. If you make it important, every step is a difficulty. Comfort becomes the paramount thing in your life. So to be a sadhu or a sanyasi means he has consciously worked to make physicality minimal in his life. He looks down on the physical. He doesn't value the physical. He doesn't see physical as a means; he is seeing it as a trap that he has to break away from.

So one basic thing is how you hold your body. What's the relationship between you and the body? Or do you have a relationship at all? There are two ways of not having a relationship. One thing is you're very separate from it. Another is, you have become it. If you have become it, then every little discomfort is a great thing. If you become separate from it, nothing matters. If you hold a distant relationship, certain things matter, but a lot of things that matter to other people don't matter to you anymore.

Already you are becoming like that. Probably a year ago, you couldn't sit cross-legged like this, with all the pain in your knees, for one or two hours, isn't it? See, slowly you are learning to hold the body a little away. Body is screaming, knees are screaming and saying, 'Hell with the satsangh, let's go!' (*Laughter*) But you have become like this: 'It's okay...' Slowly, body becomes less and less important. As body becomes less and less important, all the undulations of life don't affect you any more, because all the undulations are only for the body. When I say 'the body', it includes the mind. It's only the physical and mental bodies which are affected by the ups and downs of life, isn't it?

Once you become less and less of body, there are no undulations for you. Whichever way it is, you are only going upward. You go only one way. You don't go this way, or that way. You simply go the way you want to go, because as physicality loses its grip on you, you take charge of life. If physicality has a grip over you, you are never in control of your life.

The physical is ruled by too many forces. Nobody can ever understand it fully, nor can you ever control it. It doesn't matter how much technology you have, you will never ever control the physical a hundred per cent. We are sitting here right now. How many forces are working upon us physically? Do you know? See, the planet is round; we should be actually falling off, but we are not falling off. Not only is it round; it's spinning at a tremendous speed. We should be flying off the planet, but we are not. And the whole solar system is moving at a tremendous speed, but nothing is happening to us. There are too many forces working on the physical, too many. To keep the structure of these three particles of the atom together, do you know how many million forces are working? Too many; we will never control all of them.

So the only way to take charge of life is to distance yourself from the physical. Once you distance yourself from the physical, you are in complete charge of your life, hundred per cent.

Seeker: How do you do it?

Sadhguru: With a kitchen knife. (*Laughter*)

That is the yoga that we have been doing. But because you are a part-time yogi... (*Laughter*) Usually part-time means at least a few hours, isn't it? If you say I am doing a part-time job, does it mean twenty minutes? (*Laughter*) No, it means at least four-five hours a day you are doing the job, isn't it? So you are not even a part-time yogi. But at least if you become a part-time yogi, if for a few hours a day you are focusing on what to do with your interiority, then it'll happen very quick. If you do only twenty minutes yoga, it will still happen, but it'll take a longer time because you are taking small doses. With such a small dose it'll take much longer. If you increase the dosage, it'll work fast.

So those of you who think that you have a million year life span can go slowly. Those of you who know that they have a very short lifespan, those of you who are already grey, must hasten up, because it's a very brief life. There is no time to go in small doses. You should increase the dosage.

'A yogi can create a whole universe in his cave.'

Seeker: Why do yogis generally select hilly areas and mountains for their austerities?

Sadhguru: Just to avoid you... (*Laughs*) Just to avoid contact with you, just to stay away from you and people like you.

Now, why do they choose the mountains? Why not plains?

Why not valleys? Why not the coast? Why generally the hills? First of all, they are always looking for small enclosures. Don't think of a yogi in terms of somebody who is twisting his body. A yogi is somebody who is re-creating life completely within himself and outside of himself. See, he always wants a place that is small in size, which is compact, where he can create his own kind of energy, and where he can create his own kind of world. If you look at a yogi's cave, in your perception, it is just a little thing — maybe a ten-by-ten small hole to crawl into. But in his experience it's bigger than the world, because time and space is an illusion created by your mind. What is small and what is big, what is this much and what is that much, what is now and what is then, is all an illusion of the mind. Once a person has transcended this limitation, he can create a whole universe in his cave.

So a mountain means it's a place where earth has risen up in some way. If you bore a hole like this and try to stay in it, you won't be comfortable for many reasons. So the only place where you will find caves are in the mountains where on all sides you are enveloped with earth. That's the only place; otherwise you will have to dig a well and live in it. If you dig a well, you must slowly become a frog, because it will fill up eventually. So the only place one can live where one is surrounded by earth is a mountain. That is the reason why yogis always choose mountains, and not valleys, not plains. For their work it's important to be surrounded by earth. That's why, you know we built the Dhyanalinga temple; it's like a mound of earth and it's surrounded by earth. That's the nearest thing we could do.

When I went to Kentucky in the United States, I went to a place called Mammoth Caves. This cave can easily seat ten-to-twenty thousand people. It's huge. No columns, nothing. Just a natural cave. It's easily about ten acres sitting space; or even more probably. When I saw these Mammoth Caves, I just thought if we had a cave like this (*Laughs*), we could have consecrated it so powerfully, you know? So the nearest thing that we could come up with that is surrounded by earth is our Dhyanalinga dome. The lingam is surrounded by earth because that's the best way to keep it. A yogi wants to keep himself in that kind of situation where he is surrounded by earth. A mountain is the only natural topography which offers a certain opportunity.

'The whole art of being a guru is just this: to constantly puncture people's egos and still manage to remain their friend.'

Seeker: I've often wondered about this. What is the difference between saints, seers, sadhus and enlightened beings?

Sadhguru: Saint: Class A. Enlightened: Class B. (*Laughter*)

When you say a saint, you mean a being who has attained to a certain level of pleasantness. Saints are good people.

They are very pleasant people. But they are no good as gurus. They can only bless you. It's from that perspective in Indian culture that you bow down whenever you see a saint. Because he has a certain pleasant energy about himself, he will bless you, which will add to your life in some way. But he can't take you to your ultimate well-being. He can bless you. Many people's blessings together offer fuel for you to go on. So wherever you see a holy man or somebody saintly, you bow down to him to receive a little bit of blessing. This has been the tradition, isn't it? When you bow down to him, you don't believe he is going to be your guru or anything. You want to receive a little blessing; that's the whole idea. He's a kind of pleasant energy. Saints are very pleasant and nice people.

Yogis are a different kind. As I have said before, they are evolved in their technology. A yogi knows all the technicalities – that is, if he is a real yogi who has reached a certain attainment. If he is a practitioner of yoga, he is different. You are a practitioner of yoga right now. But if you become a yogi, that means you have experienced the oneness of existence. That means you know the intricacies of life, you know how to work it. But still a yogi may not yet be enlightened. He might have known moments of yoga or union. So if you have known moments of union in your Bhava Spandana or something, we can say you are a part-time yogi. (*Laughter*)

If you talk about a 'seer', a seer may not be spiritual at all.

He is somebody who has vision. You can put him more in the class of occult. But generally, saints and seers may be the same people. At present, I am just talking about the words. If you say 'a seer', he is somebody who is able to see things that normally people cannot see. So he has a higher level of perception. How much higher? There is no description. Even if he is one step above you, he is still a seer, yes? He is able to see one thing more than what you can see, so he is still a seer for you, as far as you are concerned.

So to come now to what you call an 'enlightened being'. The word 'enlightenment' in English has become, you know, very weak. But in the context in which we are using the word right now, enlightenment means someone has reached his ultimate point of evolution. Generally, those who reach this cannot retain their body. One cannot retain his body once he has reached his ultimate point of evolution because now keeping the physical becomes difficult. Unless he knows all the technicalities, all the nuts and bolts of how this body is made, and how to hold on to it, he cannot keep it.

So only those who get enlightened on the path of kriya are usually capable of keeping the body. If they get enlightened some other way, then they will have to use just desire — conscious desire — as a way to keep the body. There is no other way.

Seeker: How does one identify an enlightened being?

Sadhguru: Oh, it's very easy; lights will be flashing. (*Laughter*)

Why should you identify one? (*Laughter*) Where is the need for you to make a judgment that this one is enlightened, this one is not? It's not necessary for you to make that judgment. If you find that being with the man who is sweeping the street right now is helpful for you, be with him. Whether he is enlightened or not, what's your problem? It's the same thing everywhere. If you find it's nourishing for you, if it is bringing more clarity for you, if it is in some way helping you to grow, be here. If it is not, what does it matter whether I am enlightened or not? If I am enlightened but not useful for you, you should not stay. You should go, isn't it?

So instead of wasting your time trying to make a judgment about whether somebody is enlightened or not, you just see whether somebody's presence is truly useful for you or not. When I say truly useful, I mean is someone helping you to become big, or is somebody helping you to become nothing? If someone is helping you to become big, you should not be there. If someone is just making you feel good about everything, you should not be there. If someone is not letting you sit anywhere, if he breaks whatever you hold as sacred, if he never lets you rest, you must be with that one. Someone who lets you rest is not a useful presence. If you want to rest, if you want to be where you are, you can do it to yourself, isn't it? Yes or no? If you want to enter spaces, to move into dimensions that you cannot do by yourself, that is where you need another, isn't it? If you want to move into areas that you have not known and you cannot know by yourself, only then a guru is useful for you. If he is going to just offer you solace and keep you in comfort, I think you can do it yourself.

'No,' some say, 'but my guru is very loving...' If you want somebody very loving, you must get yourself a dog. (*Laughter*) Yes? Unconditionally loving, he is. If that's all you're looking for – and people are always looking for such things – I am just offering you practical solutions. If you want someone who is truly loving towards you all the time, someone who will wag his tail no matter what you do, get yourself a dog, not a guru.

If you want somebody who will never let you sit down, who will somehow – whether you are willing or unwilling – just keep you moving, only then you should seek a guru. Otherwise you will end up in the hands of charlatans who will keep you in comfort. All you need is a loving smile and nice words. I told you, get yourself a dozen dogs; they will lick you all over and make you feel good. (*Laughter*) Is it not true? For one moment they will not allow you to miss love; they will lick you from head to toe and make you feel wanted. So if you are looking for attention, if you are looking for love, if you are looking for comfort, you should not even think about who is enlightened. These gurus are horrible people. They are alive and they are dead at the same time. (*Laughs*) So people who are alive and dead at the same time, have no concern for your knees paining because they have no concern for their own knees paining. They have no concern for anybody's knee pain.

So don't look for enlightened people. Even if you think somebody is enlightened, in what way does it change your life? You think I am enlightened; in what way does it change your life? It doesn't, does it? Maybe you can go and tell your friend, 'I've found an enlightened being.' Another achievement in your life, like 'I bought a new house.' It's of no value to your life – you finding somebody and labeling them as enlightened. Are you moving on? That's of value. Are you breaking your limitations? From where you are, have you broken at least a few limitations? That's the question.

Don't look for enlightened people. Seek discomfort. Not necessarily physical discomfort. See, if you make friends, what kind of people do you make friends with? Somebody with whom you are comfortable, isn't it? What kind of people are you comfortable with, hmm? Can you get along with someone who is just like you? (*Laughter*) Is it possible? If someone is just like you, can you get along with them? They must be very different from you, but they must listen to you. (*Laughter*) This is a very serious problem. They must be very different from you, but they must listen, always. They must be very vibrant, very exciting, wild, but they must take instructions from you. (*Laughter*) Isn't it? (*Laughs*)

One day, Shankaran Pillai told his girlfriend, 'You remind me of the sea.' She got very excited. She said, 'Why? Is it because I am exciting, wild and unlimited?' He said, 'No, because you make me sick.' (*Laughter*)

So, if you look, you will always look for something that's convenient for you, comfortable for you. What is convenient for you? Whatever reinforces your ego is always comfortable and convenient for you. Anything that threatens it is not convenient for you, isn't it? So your friends are people who in many ways reinforce your ego; they always make you feel you are great, you are right. If anybody punctures your ego, he becomes your enemy. He need not necessarily do anything bad to you, but if he punctures your ego, he becomes your enemy.

Now the whole art of being a guru is just this: to constantly puncture people's egos and still manage to remain their friend. (*Laughter*) Very hard job, very difficult job, isn't it?

Part Two

Life as Pilgrimage
Uttarkashi, Guptakashi,
Tapovan

'If you walk through this life thinking too much of yourself, you're a vandal. If you take every step of your life in gratitude, if you see how small you are, you walk on this planet gently, like a pilgrim. This life could be your pilgrimage.'

As the journey unfolds, there are questions. Questions about the significance of sacred places and shrines, about spiritual masters, the path, the destination and about the purpose of the journey itself.

Set against a changing montage of picturesque backdrops — from Uttarkashi, the temple town on the banks of the river Bhagirathi, to Tapovan, the hallowed spot above the Gangotri glacier — this chapter explores a gamut of queries.

In response, Sadhguru talks of the fascinating similarities and differences between the spiritual climate of the Uttarkashi, Guptakashi and Tapovan temples. He speaks of Agastya, the great sage and father of the ancient lineage of kriya yogis, and his unique method of consecration. He speaks of his own visit to the Himalayas in a previous lifetime. He talks of how every spiritual master calculates the consequences of his spiritual legacy for centuries to come. He speaks of fascinating attempts down yogic history to create a perfect being, the 'ultimate redeemer of humanity'. He speaks of the astonishing process of alchemy — honed to a fine art in India — of transforming a rock into a god. He speaks of occult, and its intersections with modern technology. He speaks of Kali and the endangered cults of the feminine. And he talks of other subjects, from environmental degradation to human disease, from the role of emotion in spiritual growth to the importance of compassion.

With Sadhguru, the excursion is never just a devotional temple tour. It is a chance to understand the spiritual anatomy of a sacred landscape, its every nut and bolt. It is a chance to demystify ancient inherited traditions and penetrate to their underlying relevance.

It is also a chance to turn from a tourist into a pilgrim.

'Pilgrimage is a process which… makes you realize you are so small, and the more a human being willingly becomes small, the larger he becomes.'

What is the purpose of a pilgrimage? People go on tours, people trek and climb mountains because they want to achieve something; they want to conquer something; they want to enhance their life. But the purpose of a pilgrimage is to humble yourself.

People travel for various reasons. Explorers have traveled to conquer and to know. Vagabonds have traveled because they couldn't stand home (*Laughter*), and, of course, the tourists have traveled because they needed a break from their work or their family (*Laughter*). But a pilgrimage is of a different nature. You don't do a pilgrimage because you want to conquer, or you want to explore, or you want to know something. A pilgrimage is a process of humbling yourself. A pilgrimage is a process of letting something else overwhelm you.

So why we have chosen the Himalayas for a pilgrimage is that you can't help but feel small. That's one thing that must happen. You can't help it. It doesn't matter how capable you are, you can't help feeling very small in the Himalayas. If you opened your eyes and looked around, you would feel very, very small. How the ants must feel in your

home – that's how you feel when you are in the Himalayas.
You are just a tiny creature. And that's the purpose of the
pilgrimage – to know your place in this existence; to know
that you are like a particle of dust in this existence.

To know and to experience that you are so small – that is
the basic purpose of the pilgrimage. It is also to celebrate
that smallness: that we are so tiny, but still if we are willing,
we can contain the whole within ourselves. That's the beauty
of being a human being. Who is trying to act big? Is
somebody in the bus acting big? (*Laughter*) Are they? There
will always be somebody. When somebody tries to act big,
he becomes small, isn't it? If somebody does not realize how
small he is, he will fail to include everything within himself.
If he thinks he is big, he becomes small. If he knows that
he is small, he becomes unlimited. That's the beauty of
being a human being, and that's also the struggle that
human beings are going through. In their effort to become
big, they become small.

The pilgrimage is a process which helps you in that
direction. It makes you realize you are so small, and the more
a human being willingly becomes small, the larger he
becomes. The more he is willing to lay himself down as
nothing, he becomes very, very big. He really becomes
boundless.

Every human being is looking for the same thing, but just
looking in the wrong direction. Everybody wants to become

boundless. In that effort, they tried to become big, and they became very small, petty human beings. Nothing wrong with their intention; just the wrong direction, that's all. It takes lots of awareness for one to see that in dissolving yourself, you become big. It's not in trying to become big that you become big. To realize that, to know that, unfortunately, for most people takes lifetimes. Just for four people to be in one place is such a difficulty, isn't it? Yes? Just for two people to be in one place is such a difficulty, isn't it? Because who is bigger than who is always the question. Once people are making an effort to be big, they become pettier and pettier. They will start doing more and more idiotic things in their lives. Wherever human beings are trying to be big, that is where the most stupid things happen.

Science, technology and human ingenuity are wonderful, but those who are truly involved in technology know how small it is compared to existence. The high-end scientists know how small our technology is, but those who are using the technology start believing that they are very big. Just because we are driving a bus or a car and we can cover incredible distances, we tend to lose perspective of what's what around us.

But I don't want you to lose that perspective. I want you to experience this as a pilgrimage, not as a tour. There is a huge difference between going to a place as a pilgrim, and going to the same place as a tourist. Maybe you've been oscillating between the two (*Laughs*). At times you have the

steadiness of a pilgrim. But when you see a dirty bathroom
or (*Laughs*) the steepness of the mountain, maybe you
become a tourist. A pilgrim's goal is set. No matter what,
that is where he is going; life or death, that's where he is
going. A tourist is not like that; a tourist is going only to
comfortable places. Nothing wrong with that. It's just that
when we live with certain limitations, life imposes its own
limitations. Only within yourself when you live without any
limitations, life opens up its bounty for you.

Going through the Himalayas should leave you as nothing.
When you approach life, if you are able to become nothing,
or something very small, you will become a very wonderful
human being. If you approach life and people as a very big
man or woman, then you become an utterly ugly human
being. If you walk through this life thinking too much of
yourself, you're a vandal. If you take every step of your life
in gratitude, if you see how small you are, you walk on this
planet gently, like a pilgrim. This life could be your
pilgrimage.

These mountains have drawn people for thousands of years.
Now the numbers have increased because of easier ways to
travel. But otherwise, even in the ancient past, people came
every year. Those who were realized came to the mountains
just to escape the people, but people followed. Now
especially, there is no escape because there are roads
everywhere. Probably, as the roads get better and better,
everybody will vacation in the Himalayas. (*Laughs*) In one

way, it's good, but in another way, it's not good at all!

'When we walk the path of kriya, we naturally say we belong to the lineage of Agastya – not to claim a pedigree, but just to express gratitude to a man who was so much larger than life.'

Seeker: Sadhguru, I wanted to know more about the Uttarkashi Temple we went to in the morning. Why were there three lingas outside the shrine?

Sadhguru: Oh, that's because this place is ancient. As I told you, it was built 4,225 years ago.

(*Laughs*) Yesterday I asked some people to touch the main linga at a particular point, and see what it feels like. So they went and touched it and said, 'The rest of the place feels different but this feels very familiar.' I said, 'What is it that is so familiar to you? Feel it again and see what is so familiar to you.' Then they felt it again and again and said, 'Something very familiar. We can't say what; it's so familiar. What is it?' Then after much thinking, they said, 'It feels like you.' I was laughing. The moment you mention this temple, I feel like laughing because (*Laughs*) whoever created this – I didn't go into the details of this; some day we could – could be Agastya himself. I don't know. It could be him, or someone as wonderful as him.

You've heard of Agastya muni? Among the Sapta Rishis,

among the seven direct disciples of Shiva who started the
process of yoga, Agastya is the ultimate in kriya yoga. If
you say 'kriya,' it means Agastya; it's like that. So everybody
who comes from the lineage of kriya naturally claims their
lineage to Agastya muni. Anything and everything that can
be done on the level of human energy, Agastya spoke about
it and did those things in a miraculous way. So when we
walk the path of kriya, we naturally say we belong to the
lineage of Agastya – not to claim a pedigree, but just to
express gratitude to a man who was so much larger than
life. It's very difficult for one to imagine what kind of men
these rishis were. They don't belong to this world.

So once this linga is created and the temple is around, then
people like you come along. You like to innovate, and you
want to leave your own mark on the temple, because the
main job has been already done. Some very crude people will
go to the back of the temple and write, 'Rebecca loves John.'
The crude ones do it that way, yes? Some people go with a
chalk and do it; some people go with paint and write it.
Some people will go with a chisel in India. At the back of
the temple they will chisel 'AVR loves SKP'. Have you seen
these initials? So they want to leave their own mark. Because
of this madness, anybody who had a piece of stone and a
chisel started making lingas without understanding the
science behind it, without understanding the power behind
it. Anybody who had a stone and chisel made one. It is one
of the easiest forms to make.

So why three lingas? That's your question. There are temples where there are over thousand lingas around the main linga. Everybody who came started making their own lingas to satisfy their own nonsense. They are of no significance. What is inside is of tremendous magnitude and for it to stay like it was just consecrated yesterday – the linga is as vibrant as if it was consecrated just last night – makes it an incredible job. It's beyond the human imagination as to how and with what sense, understanding and deadly accuracy things have been done. The Uttarkashi temple is another dimension by itself.

Seeker: You have said that the offering stone on the left side of the sanctum sanctorum has a certain significance. Could you tell us about it?

Sadhguru: Did you notice it? An offering stone? An eight-petalled flower? Usually, these are guru pooja stones. I won't go into all the details. You won't be able to digest it. But let me tell you one thing that may shock you. Yesterday, I just wanted to read the history of the temple on this stone. What I found, when I looked at this stone, was that people have been offering menstrual fluids to Shiva. Now that's something you can't digest. You're not even supposed to enter the temple at certain times of the month. But they have been offering menstrual fluids to the temple, to Shiva himself.

See, one of the simplest ways to do certain activity, which is beyond the physical, is with sacrifice. It could be animal sacrifice. Human sacrifice has also been in practice for a long time. A life which is in full potency and full vibrancy, if you suddenly break the body, there is a science of making use of the life energy that comes out. This is the basis of all sacrifice. So even human sacrifice has been in practice in various tantric cults in India. Already you are not able to digest it!

Now, if you don't want to kill a human being, the nearest thing to that is menstrual fluid. When your mother was pregnant she didn't have a menstrual cycle, because she was using those very menstrual fluids to make you. You've come out of that. So these people simply use it; they have no qualms about it. They just know life as life. There is no aversion, no attraction. They're like scientists. They have no morals, no religion, no values, nothing. They just know life the way it is.

And if I even say this about a major temple in the country, people will throw stones at me. But this is what they did and I laughed my head off last night when I went there. (*Laughs*) All the brahmins in the temple will turn in their graves for eternity if they just come to know this is what people have been doing.

Seeker: How are you able to decode these processes of consecration? Is it by some power of intuition?

Sadhguru: See, I have often said that intuition is only a different kind of computing. It is a means by which you arrive at the same answer as the logical process. It is just that you arrive at it more quickly, though not so surely.

All mystical knowledge comes from that dimension of existence that people are unable to access with their sense organs. This is a completely different dimension of perception. Metaphorically, it is termed the third eye. What you can see, hear, smell, taste and touch is limited. There are types of information that cannot be perceived by your eyes, ears, nose, tongue and skin. Think of a camera or a periscope; these offer you other ways of seeing. Think of ultrasonic or subsonic sound; your ears cannot hear it, but it exists. Likewise the x-ray is able to see what your eyes cannot see. Similarly, with mystical knowledge; it is about accessing a type of information that cannot be perceived by the sense organs. It is just another dimension of perception. All perception is just a gathering of information on different levels.

'I don't know any chanting; I don't know any rituals. I simply know how to switch energy from one dimension to another.'

Seeker: This question is about two places we've visited. In Guptakashi, my experience was overwhelming, and it was just as incredible in Tapovan. Just sitting in these places was indescribable. I was wondering if you could explain the significance of both these places.

Sadhguru: These are two very different kinds of places —
Guptakashi and Tapovan. In Tapovan, maybe because of the
altitude you felt light-headed. It is a place that has been
graced by many wonderful beings. Wherever they go, they
leave their eggs; that's their way of life. Now, if you leave
your eggs in Bombay, or in New York City or anywhere else,
people will trample on them and go, because they won't have
the sense to recognize what's been left around. So these
beings go and leave their eggs in remote places.

And similarly, the yogis — people who have the privilege and
the burden of carrying a dimension which is not in the
experience of common people — also lay their eggs wherever
they sit and stand. But why they always moved to hilly
regions and to certain spaces which are identified as sacred,
is simply so that these eggs are not trampled upon, but
rather experienced, made use of, so that something will fly
out of them. Tapovan has been one bird's nest where many,
many yogis have chosen to lay their eggs. But the bigger
pits of eggs are Kedar and Kailash. In Kedar, every kind of
bird laid its eggs — multicolored eggs — and they got all
mixed up.

So if you have been initiated in a certain way, you become
open to a certain aspect of experience. There are so many
other things there which you are not open to, but if you
are initiated in a particular way, you become open to that
particular dimension. Let's say we have initiated you in the
peacock's ways, you become open to only the colors of the

peacock. A parrot is sitting right there, but you don't know that. So depending upon the type of initiations you have gone through, you become open to certain dimensions of experience.

So Tapovan is a tremendous possibility. Beyond Tapovan there is a place called Nandanvan, which is at about 17,200 or 17,400 degrees altitude, which has many eggs. I am thinking that some day, probably before I am too lazy to climb mountains, I want to go and spend a couple of weeks there and sort out a few eggs. Because my eggs are all laid in the cities where (*Laughs*) some people experience them, and some people trample them. I also want to lay some eggs which will live for a long time.

One big egg I have laid that you can't destroy is the Dhyanalinga. So that is good enough. But still I thought that I too should lay my eggs in places where they will remain for a long time, where people will approach them with a certain reverence and become available to them. Suppose I lay my eggs on Times Square, people who are walking there are not walking with an openness to be able to experience that. In spite of this, there maybe somebody who may be hit by them. But that's rare because everyone is going with self-protection on. Self-preservation is the biggest thing when you are walking on the street.

Now if you go to Tapovan, you are going with a certain reverence, a certain openness that makes it a possibility. This is the whole basis of creating temples in India: a certain kind of egg is laid and you are supposed to approach it in a certain way, so that the experience becomes a possibility for you. For every deity, there is a certain type of approach. So Tapovan is not as complex as Kedar, but is still a complex mixture of things.

Guptakashi is a wonderful place; the consecration of the linga has been done very wonderfully. This is an area where Agastya muni walked; he probably even visited this temple – either he himself or one of his people. The nature of the linga is in line with Agastya's way of doing things, which is pure kriya, or hundred per cent energy work. No other things: no mantras, no tantras, nothing; it's hundred per cent energy work. That's the way I am. That's the only thing I know. I can just transform life from one dimension to another, simply on the basis of energy. I don't know any chanting; I don't know any rituals. I simply know how to switch energy from one dimension to another.

You know what Guptakashi means? 'Gupt' means secret. And Kashi or Varanasi is the holiest of holy cities; one of the most ancient cities of learning. This was a place where hundreds of enlightened beings lived at a time. Every street you walked on, you had an enlightened being to meet. So it became a tradition in this culture that if you want to die, you must die in Kashi. If you die in Kashi, your liberation is guaranteed because there are so many enlightened ones who every day come to have a bath in the Ganga. All you have to do is just have a glimpse of them, and when they see that your time is near, definitely they will help you, and you're through. So even today it is believed when you come to a certain age, you should travel to Kashi and wait there to die. Mass cremations will happen on the river bank. Even now, you must go to this Manikarnika Ghat. A dozen bodies will be burning right there, and a dozen bodies will be waiting in queue. That sounds horrible to you?

Most of them have come to die in Kashi. A few of them have died elsewhere and the relatives have brought them to Kashi because these are people who believe. You know even if somebody dear to you is dead, you still take them to the hospital, isn't it? Yes? Just in case. (*Laughs*) So just like that, people who have emotions do these things. They bring dead bodies and burn them in Kashi, hoping that something will happen. This tradition came simply because every generation saw hundreds of enlightened beings living in Kashi and it became the greatest centre of learning.

So Kashi means the holiest of the holy. And that is where we went yesterday. What we left this morning is Uttarkashi. Uttarkashi means the northern Kashi. What we went the other day, just after Kedar, is Guptakashi, the 'secret Kashi'. Nobody is supposed to know about it. All these Kashis have very powerful lingas which are referred to as jyotirlingas. They are self-created; they were not created by anybody; they grew out of the earth in the form of a linga. People recognized them and worked upon them to make them into something else. So this is Guptakashi because it is very much in line with Agastya's way.

So for our meditators, for people who have been initiated in the Isha way, Guptakashi would be very vibrant and available because I have laid my eggs there, lots of them. So that space is always more conducive for our people; they will be more receptive to that kind of thing. Uttarkashi would be a very different proposition for you because it belongs to a completely different world, although somebody who touched the linga said it felt just like me. (*Laughs*) Yes, it is true, but that face of me you have not seen yet.

'We mystics are not civilized people...'

Seeker: You have said that there is only one contemporary mystic, other than you, with three lifetimes as an enlightened being behind him. On August 29, 2007, you said he had attained mahasamadhi. How did you know of this being? Did you ever meet him?

Sadhguru: Yes, there was such a yogi. Once when I was in Guptakashi, I realized that he was in that region. But there was no need for me to meet him. Why should I? Haven't I seen enough? If we came face to face, we'd probably be embarrassed. But I knew about him and he knew about me. I always keep myself well informed about the competition!

Seeker: So you never met him when you came to the Himalayas?

Sadhguru: We did meet. But when and where doesn't matter. When and where are just your creations.

Seeker: And what happened when you met?

Sadhguru: We looted each other's bags of attainment. When I didn't find anything new, I stepped back. He probably didn't find anything either. There was nothing we needed to know in terms of realization. But there is always something to know in terms of attainment or capability. So we looted each other's bags, found nothing new and stepped back.

Seeker: But why would you need to loot someone else's 'bag'?

Sadhguru: See, if you've been a seeker of truth, it's just a matter of habit to check out each other's attainments. For instance, only an unread person would ignore a new book; for a person who reads, it's impossible not to check out a new book in a bookstore. Similarly, an adept wants to look at all the possibilities. The nature of enlightenment is such that one could always learn something more. In civilized terms, we could call it an 'exchange'. But because we mystics are not civilized people, we prefer to call it 'looting'.

Seeker: Why uncivilized? Is there any force or violence involved in raiding each other's bags of attainment?

Sadhguru: No force. Neither of us puts up any barriers. But there's nothing civilized about a mystic. He remains very consciously uncivilized. Civilization is what you pick up from outside. If a mystic picked up things from outside he wouldn't be a mystic. He'd be a mistake. That's what our priests, pundits and mullahs are — just an accumulated cacophony of culture and civilization.

Seeker: I understand that in a previous lifetime as Sadhguru Sri Brahma, you actually visited Guptakashi?

Sadhguru: Yes, over seventy years ago, Sadhguru Sri Brahma came here. He came with four young men; he wanted to assist them in a certain sadhana. They walked about eighty-five kilometers from Rudraprayag to Kedar. They were planning to stay there for a long time. But they were not prepared for the cold; they had come from a much warmer climate in South India.

Then, food was also a problem. Just this morning, when we sat for the afternoon meal, I was telling somebody that in this lifetime, wherever I go — even if I go unprepared — food has always been there for me. After three lifetimes of having a hard time with food, this time around food is always there, any part of the world I go. (*Laughs*) Food is not a big thing, but when you don't have it, it can become a big thing. One aspect of Indian spirituality has always been about walking and not eating. So when you become extremely hungry, you tend to become like an animal. When food comes in front of you, you will fight, you will kill, you will do anything for it. But to be in extreme hunger and to maintain absolute dignity, that's one part of the sadhana.

So Sadhguru came with these four boys to Kedar, but the weather didn't allow them to continue what they wanted to do. So they chose this place in Guptakashi. They walked back here and stayed here in this temple for close to two months. In this lifetime, I returned with two disciples. Six years ago when we came here, two of those boys were here with us in different forms. One of them is now a woman. They were here with us in this same temple. That was an incredible situation. The other two are no more with us.

So this place has been dear to me in some way because it sheltered us and kept us going. Every time we come to Himalayas we just spend a little time here and go.

'I know the consequence of my teaching perfectly well. I am not teaching something impulsively.'

Seeker: So when these various gurus or exalted beings laid what you call their 'eggs' in various places, they were planning well into the future. Did the Buddha do the same? Did he know what would happen to his legacy centuries afterwards? And what about you, Sadhguru?

Sadhguru: Yes, he did. I want you to understand Gautama is a master; Gautama is a guru who knows the consequence of his teaching perfectly well. So am I. I know the consequence of my teaching perfectly well. I am not teaching something impulsively.

If I (*Laughs*) tell you the various aspects of my life, the impossible complications, and with what deadly accuracy I am going at it, you will feel I am ruthless probably – or you will think I am God himself. It's up to you what you decide, but there is a consequence to everything, including the teaching, because the teaching is a karma. A method is a karma; it's an activity. When you perform this karma, there is a consequence. So the consequence always needs to be calculated; there is no perfect consequence for any action. Only a fool believes that something is good, something is bad. No, every action has a consequence and the consequence is never perfect. You just have to see whether you are ready for the consequence or not, that's all.

Especially when you perform spiritual activity, the consequence is there in a very huge way. So what is the consequence that you will create in the next hundred, two hundred, five hundred years, is something that every guru has to look at. Why all these many wonderful yogis and mystics in the Himalayas never uttered a teaching is simply because of that. They looked at the consequence, and they were unwilling to face the consequence of their actions. So they decided not to act; they just left their energies in a certain way, which also has its consequence, but very minimal. That's the reason why they chose to perform that kind of action which doesn't involve anybody except themselves. They just invested themselves in different ways. Somebody's open to experience it, somebody's not open. If even a donkey walks through it, it's okay; a mountaineer walks through it, it's okay; a devotee comes and he explodes, it is okay. Whichever way, it is okay. That is a very sensible thing to do. But now, once you take to teaching, you have to see what the consequence is.

Gautama said, 'If I initiate only monks, this spiritual process will last for two thousand five hundred years; but if I initiate women, the lifespan of what I am doing will come down by two thousand years.' Is it because there is something wrong with women? That is not the point. It is just a consequence. Now men and women come and sit here for spiritual purposes; when the guru is there, they are inspired; they forget who is man, who is woman. But when the guru goes away, then they start looking around, and being a man and woman becomes very dominant. After that, there will be no spirituality; there will be just men and women. To just have men and women, you don't have to have a spiritual group; you can have that on the street. So Gautama is right in saying that. There's nothing wrong with it.

He aspired that his teaching should last for a long time, so he made his teaching very dry. He squeezed all the juice out of it. It's the dryness of the teaching which has made it last so long. If it was very lively and juicy, it would be absolutely misinterpreted by now. Though its lasted this long, terrible misinterpretations to Gautama's teachings have still happened.

Now in the case of Isha, with this process, in a very active way, it will last for six hundred to seven hundred years. After that, in a lowered way it will last. But the energy part of it is indestructible. It's forever; nobody can destroy it. That's the reason my activity is balanced between the two. Though right now in Isha, the teaching looks like the major part, in my life, it is actually just a small part. The real work that I do is not in what I am speaking, in what I am doing around the world. The real work is that I am constantly laying eggs which can't be destroyed, which will be there forever.

As long as the energy aspect of the work is maintained, the moment the right kind of individual or individuals arrive and are touched by the energy — even if it's a thousand years later — the spiritual process will be rejuvenated. If nobody of that caliber comes along, the spiritual process will last around six hundred to seven hundred years. But if someone does come, who knows how long he will make it last? He could use the same seed, and make another kind of garden out of it. One gardener may be able to make his garden yield five hundred mangoes; another may know how to make it yield five thousand.

There was a bishop on the east coast of America in the 1890s. He went to Ohio for a conference where he met a young minister who was substituting for a physics professor in the university.

The bishop said, 'I believe the end of the world is near, because everything that man can possibly do has been done.'

The minister said, 'That's not true. In the next fifty years, man will invent more than ever before. Why, man may even be able to fly.'

The bishop rejected that idea. He said, 'Flying is the angels' domain.'

Fifteen years later, Wilbur and Orville flew the world's first airplane — and they happened to be the bishop's sons. So who knows what capabilities someone will bring to Isha in the future?

'Transmission is much more important than teaching. Teaching is only a way of knocking on the door.'

Seeker: And what about the past? Is Isha itself the culmination of many centuries of spiritual effort?

Sadhguru: Forty thousand years ago, there lived a Himalayan yogi named Sunira in modern-day Nepal. We believe he belonged to just the next generation after the

Sapta Rishis – the seven sages. He was an incredible guru but he was still not happy with himself.

He took on an impossible project. He wanted to create a kind of being who is absolutely perfect. So he took up the project of creating such a being. So synthetic stuff is not of the twentieth or twenty-first century's making! Way back, Sunira wanted to create a synthetic being who would become a perfect teacher; who would become the ultimate redeemer of humanity. An impossible project, but Sunira was a man of incredible capability. So he took on such a project and he started putting together a being with every kind of quality that you can think of. This longing must have come because this was just after Shiva, the Adi Yogi, left. They must have been missing him so badly that the longing to create a perfect being must have been a natural longing. This must have seemed like a natural project to take up.

When Sunira's disciples saw what a phenomenal project he was undertaking, they were hugely impressed by their master's capabilities. He worked through his lifetime to create this perfect being, and towards the end of his life when this dream remained unfulfilled, Sunira made a prophecy. He said, 'The essence of what I have started will find fulfillment and reverberate – not here, not now, but much later in the green hills of the south – and then it will reach the world.' The Velliangiri hills are green, and (*Laughs*) we are in the south...

It has been a long term project among mystics and yogis down the ages to create this perfect synthetic being – later called Maitreya – capable of making the whole world conscious. So generation after generation, yogis tried to continue the same half-finished project of Sunira. It's always been [going on] in the yogic lore. But in the last century, it came to social knowledge because the Theosophists worked on it. Annie Besant, Leadbeater and Madame Blavatsky took this project up, and said they were going to make it. They amassed a vast amount of occult knowledge. Probably for the first time in the last few hundred years, and definitely for the first time in a modern way, they took up this unfinished project. They had the knowledge but they did not have the capability. They acquired much information but they could not acquire the necessary means to do anything like that. So they made desperate attempts to declare that it had happened. Twice they made serious efforts to simply declare that they had completed the project and that the perfect being had come. But it did not work.

Another parallel effort has also been made for the last couple of millennia by another set of yogis who were aware of Sunira's glorious-but-quite-impossible project. And with their wisdom, they started working upon a similar force to create a similar possibility, but with a completely different understanding of the same. The fruition of that parallel line of creating a perfect being (but not as a human being) is the making of the Dhyanalinga.

So here sits a perfect being, but not in human form. That's because the human system has all the capabilities but still doesn't have the necessary integrity of boundary to hold it. I think I have said many times that the Dhyanalinga has all the necessary ingredients; it has the energy body of a perfect being. In theory, we can give him a physical body. In theory, it is possible. We can add flesh and blood to him and make him stand up and walk. But if he does that, he will no more be a perfect being, because then he will have to eat, he will have to excrete, he will have to sleep, he will have to wake up and rub his eyes in the morning – and people will find fault with him! (*Laughs*). 'You said you are perfect but you are eating; you said you are perfect but you are sitting; you said you are perfect but you are standing; you said you are perfect but you are sleeping!' So it is best he remains this way.

Sitting here on the occasion of Guru Poornima, almost ten years after he's come into reality, is significant, because in every way he is a perfect being and a perfect guru. I am saying he is a perfect guru because he doesn't bother you like me. (*Laughs*) If you are willing, he is all there; if you are not willing, he is simply not there; that's perfect. I am not like that. Whether you are willing or not willing I am after you. (*Laughs*) So Sunira's prophecy has come true, but not the way he thought it would.

Seeker: Do you mean that the Dhyanalinga is the long-envisaged Maitreya?

Sadhguru: Maitreya is still a half-done man. Masters have been trying to build this being for a long time. Many mystics have added substance to him but he has never been completed.

But southern mysticism has brought another kind of intelligence to this project. People always thought a perfect being would walk and teach. But he doesn't have to. The Dhyanalinga sits in one place and he transmits. He won't walk; he won't teach; he just sits and transmits. Transmission is much more important than teaching. Teaching is only a way of knocking on the door. All gurus transmit – and after all, all yogis are meant to sit! The Dhyanalinga does both. He is a perfect being without the frailties of being human.

Seeker: How did you find out about Sunira's project? Did you read about it somewhere?

Sadhguru: How do I know? The news is being broadcast all the time, and I also happened to hear it. As there is an internet, there is also an 'inner-net'. All the work that has been ever done in the realm of consciousness lives. And it can be accessed.

'There is a whole technology of transforming a piece of rock into a god.'

Seeker: Sadhguru, could you explain the difference between a live temple and a dead temple? You can see that the priests sometimes exploit the whole business of ritual and worship. Or is the shraddha or faith of hordes of devotees enough to keep the place alive? Does a live temple ever die?

Sadhguru: It all depends on the method and the process of consecration. The most popular way of consecrating was always a ritualistic way, using mantras and rituals. If it is done this way, it needs a periodic rejuvenation process, with the right kind of people and the right kind of processes. If that doesn't happen, the temple will slowly die. But if it is consecrated by other means – other than rituals – then, no matter what kind of person is around, what kind of situation is around, you cannot kill that place anymore. For example, at the Dhyanalinga, or even Kedar, even if the most terrible people lived there, you could not kill those temples. But if it is consecrated with rituals, it needs constant maintenance and rejuvenation of proper ritualistic processes. Otherwise, it will die.

Seeker: What energy was the Dhyanalinga consecrated for? Was it for prosperity or was it for a different purpose?

Sadhguru: What did you go there for? (*Laughter*)

Seeker: I just went. I didn't go expecting any particular energy. I didn't know there was a different energy for different temples.

Sadhguru: See, Dhyanalinga is multidimensional; that's what is unique about it. It has been consecrated with all the seven basic chakras, all the seven different dimensions of life.

And the significant part is that this is done with solidified mercury, which modern chemistry does not believe is possible at room temperature. Normally, if mercury has to be solidified, it has to be minus thirty-two degrees centigrade; otherwise you cannot solidify mercury. But you will see a huge piece of mercury there. It is just two feet tall, what you can see, but it weighs 682 kilograms, because mercury is the only substance which can weigh that much on this planet. And it's solidified mercury at room temperature. This is a certain Indian alchemy which is known as 'rasavaidya' through which you solidify mercury and create these things. The material chosen and the form that is chosen is such that you can give it whatever kind of reverberation you want and it will retain it for a very long time, almost forever.

There is a whole technology of transforming a piece of rock into a god. What you call 'god' right now, if you want to look at it this way, is just energy, reverberating in so many different ways. If it's reverberating in a particular way, you call it a rock. If it's reverberating in a different way, you call it a tree. If it is reverberating in another way, you call it an animal; another way you call it a human being. It simply means it's the same energy expressing itself in different ways.

A gross form of expression is something very physical like a rock. The subtlest form of expression, you can call it the divine.

So the art of consecration is to transform what is gross to the subtlest possible level. So we are not talking about bringing a god down. We are talking about transforming this piece of flesh and bone into a godlike entity by itself. That which you right now refer to as human can become divine by doing the right kind of things within the same system. So if you can make a rock reverberate like the divine, definitely you can make this one (*referring to the self*) reverberate like the divine, isn't it? Because it's the same energy; it is just in different levels of operation, different levels of manifestation and expression.

Seeker: So the energy of the Dhyanalinga is that of a human being?

Sadhguru: It is, because it has come with all the seven chakras. You can say that it is a live person without a physical body. This is too far-fetched, too much mumbo-jumbo, but in theory, as I've said before, it's possible: if we want, we can build a physical body for him. But then, what's the point? Once you build a physical body, he comes with all the limitations of the physical body. Right now he is fine without the physical body. He reverberates very powerfully. No physical body means no problem of time-span and all these things.

'If your energy body is in proper balance and in full flow, there is no question of disease in your body.'

Seeker: Sadhguru, when you were constructing the Dhyanalinga, you were not well and every day doctors were diagnosing different types of diseases. Does this mean that just by the disturbance of the life energy you can get different types of diseases? In our medical science, we try to find causative agents and factors for different diseases. We spend lots of money and energy to find out the cause. And here it seems that there is a common, or uncommon, factor — that is, the disturbance of the life energy. And the treatment seems to be correction of the life energy. So what is it all about?

Sadhguru: When I say 'disease', let's make a distinction between infectious diseases and chronic diseases. The infectious have come upon us because of an external invasion, for which today you doctors have invented so many chemicals. And the chemicals that you are using to kill these organisms also kill a part of you, which we are aware of today. In many ways this damages your own system. But you know, what has to be done has to be done. It's like spraying insecticides on our crops today. We know it is not healthy. At the same time we cannot stop it, because we want to eat. So we continue to use all those medicines to control the infectious diseases, because today infectious diseases are a big thing — mainly because we are living in unnecessary proximity with people.

For example, you come from Mumbai. Why have some eight million people all gathered in one place? Have you fallen in love with each other or something? Definitely you can see it's not because of love. Because of a certain sense of greed and survival instinct, people have come together like this. When people live in such close proximity – such a huge number of people – infections, or infectious diseases can play havoc with life. For that, you have evolved so many vaccines, and antibiotics and so many other kinds of poisons to kill them. These poisons not only kill them, they also damage a certain part of you. But it is a calculated risk that we take with life, and we live on.

But when it comes to a chronic ailment, whatever may be the ailment, the root cause of that ailment is always in the energy body. And your energy body functions the way it functions for various reasons. It may be because of the kind of atmosphere you live in; it may be because of the kind of food that you eat; it may be because of the kind of relationships that you hold; it may be because of your emotions; it may be because of your attitudes and thoughts and the opinions that you hold about life; it may be because of certain external energy situations that disturb your internal energy; or the physiological and psychological manifestations which disturb the energy. In some way, your energy body is disturbed, which will naturally manifest both physiologically and psychologically. It is one layer of the body, the energy body. Once it is disturbed, the mental body and the physical body are bound to be disturbed.

Actually, it becomes a doctor's concern only after it becomes a medical problem. Till then it is not a doctor's concern, because there is no physiological manifestation. For example, I have been talking about myself. Right now there is a certain disturbance in the energy body. But if I go to your doctor, he will take my blood, he will check my heart, pulse, this, that, everything – you know, all those parameters. He will say I am perfectly healthy, which I am, physiologically. But if I do not fix my energy body, I know within the next few months, things will start manifesting physiologically, in my body, as a disease. Unfortunately, medical science understands only disease. It does not understand the root of health, where it comes from, the basis of health.

Medical science is always busy studying disease. I think they should take time to study health. Human nature has always been like this: wherever the problem is, that's where you put your attention. Right now there is a disease; that's a problem, so you put your attention there. This is a very rudimentary way of thinking and functioning in the world. But unfortunately that's how the world is functioning right now: if there is a problem, you attend to it; and if there is no problem, you don't attend to it. If your energy body is in proper balance and in full flow, there is no question of disease in your body – either physiologically or psychologically. It's impossible.

Right now, on this Himalayan trek, you have been hearing people sharing their experiences. Somebody, who has a medical condition with which she can't walk any number of feet, goes up to 14,700 feet elevation, walking up an eighteen-kilometer path. Now, the first thing that people would like to call this is a miracle. I don't want this termed a miracle, because if you term it a miracle you are dismissing a whole science, a whole wisdom, a whole understanding of life. It is not a miracle; it's just another level of understanding of life and the way life happens.

Now, people are spending enormous amounts of money and resources to research into the possibilities of liberating the human race from diseases. With the advance of medical science, we have been able to contain so many infections. Almost every infection that can arise today, you have some solution for it. But look at the simple ailments which man is creating for himself, like diabetes, or blood pressure, or migraine headaches, or whatever else that he causes from within. Please see, medical science is not offering any solution for these. It is only offering to manage the diseases, never really talking about freeing you from those diseases.

Today, there are whole systems of medicine, so many kinds of specialists to manage diseases for people, to manage them within certain limitations. A lot of money and time is being spent on just managing those diseases. It is just like people talking about stress management. People want to 'manage' their stress, 'manage' their diabetes, 'manage' their blood pressure. It's ridiculous. Simply because they have not understood the fundamentals of how their own life energies function, this kind of foolishness has entered. Yes, if people are willing to do a certain amount of sadhana to balance and activate their pranamayakosha, or their energy body, they can definitely be free of all chronic ailments. Infections you have to protect yourself against, and be careful.

Seeker: The disturbance of the pranic energies produces certain kinds of diseases – that's what you indicated. Are those different from the physiological diseases that doctors normally diagnose?

Sadhguru: No, they're the same. I mentioned even the names of the diseases, so they are not different. Doctors diagnose them only when they manifest physiologically. But if the energy system is perfect, there is no question of it manifesting physiologically. Only because the energy is disturbed, it manifests physiologically. It's not different; it is the same diseases that I am talking about, but not what you contract from without – something that happened within the system.

'I am not trying to take away your gods from you. It's just that you never had them.'

Seeker: In some temples, they do something called 'prana pratishtha'*, and turn the statue into an idol. Do you think

---

* A process of consecrating or energizing an object with divine energies through a direct process involving the consecrator's own life energies.

it is worth sitting in that type of temple for some time, as
is the tradition in south India?

Sadhguru: If they have done prana pratishtha, definitely.
What I am calling consecration is pratishtha. If you have
really done prana pratishtha, definitely it will reverberate in
a very different way and people can benefit from that.

Those of you who are looking distressed, I am not trying
to take away your gods from you. It's just that you never
had them. You just believe something that has been told to
you, isn't it? And if we work hard enough on you, we can
make you believe anything – just about anything.

Seeker: Well, it is taking time to digest. (*Laughter*) This is
something in which the whole world believes; at least
something in which different faiths and cultures believe.

Sadhguru: It happened once. There were two boys, very
energetic. When young boys are very energetic, they will be
constantly in trouble, you know. They were brothers,
constantly in trouble. The whole neighborhood was talking
about them. The parents were very embarrassed that
everybody was talking about their children. So they wanted
to fix the kids. They decided they would take them to the
local parish priest. Together, the two boys were very strong.
So they decided to deal with them separately. First they took
the younger boy, left him in the priest's office and went
away.

The priest entered the office with his long robe. Dramatically he walked up and down. Very calculated drama. I want you to understand, ninety per cent of the religion runs on drama. If you take away the drama, very little is left. The boy just followed the priest doing the ping-pong act, looking at him up and down, up and down. The priest was thinking of how to make this boy give up all his mischief. He thought, if I remind this boy that God is within you, all his mischief will go away. Some stupid hope. These stupid hopes are those that only people who have not brought up children have, okay? (*Laughs*) These things have never worked, but people have hope.

So suddenly in his stride he stopped and asked, 'Where is God?' The boy looked bewildered, looked all over. He must be somewhere in the priest's office. Then the priest thought, okay, he is not getting it. He wants to give him a clue. So he pointed towards the boy and asked, 'Where is God?' He wants him to get the point – that God is within. The boy looked even more bewildered, looked under the table. No God. Then the priest thought, okay, he is not getting it. He walked across the table, came close to the boy, pointed his finger at the little boy's chest and asked, 'Where is God?' The boy just got up and bolted out of the room, ran straight to the place where his elder brother was and told him, 'We are in trouble.' His brother asked, 'Why?' He said, 'They have lost their God and they think we did it.' (*Laughter*)

I didn't take away anything; you never had it. If the divine is with you, can anybody take it away? (*Laughs*) If it can be taken away, it should be dumped immediately. Anything that can be taken away, you must dump. Then you will be left with something that cannot be taken away.

See, why do you believe something? First of all, because you are not sincere enough to admit that you do not know, isn't it? Why can't we just live life simply? What you know, you know; what you do not know, you do not know. Isn't it okay to be like this? Why should we go on believing something? It is very clear to us that with all these teachings of morality we have not really cleaned up the world in any way. In fact, people have just become more devious. Maybe if you had not talked about all these things, their focus would have been elsewhere, because this is the nature of the mind. The moment you tell somebody, don't think about this, don't do this, that's what they will do.

Right from their childhood, unnecessarily you are getting them on to all those things. What would have been just a passing interest for them has become a lifelong interest for them, because you told them these are evil things, don't touch them. How can they stay away from it? If you had just left it, each person according to his own tendencies, according to his needs, he would have found his own way, isn't it? Why don't you trust human intelligence? If you leave it to intelligence, it will find its way. There is no need to teach life to everybody. There is no need to codify life. You just leave it to people; they will find their way. You think everybody will go wild. Not true. We will come to some kind of order with that also.

So dharma was created as a lubricant for life, in a sense. See, the nature of human transactions is such that every transaction you make, what is your profit is somebody else's loss. What is his profit is your loss. This is the nature of every human transaction. When this is the nature of the transaction, every transaction is a possible friction. If there isn't a certain amount of understanding, love and some kind of lubrication, every transaction is a possible friction, isn't it? Once you are in a certain level of bitterness with somebody, do you see every little transaction becomes a friction? Only if it is lubricated with a certain amount of love, this passes easily.

To avoid this friction in daily transactions, society made certain guidelines. They are not God-given guidelines. At a particular time, to see that there is least amount of friction in family situations, in social situations, in national situations, they codified a certain transaction. This is just human sense. If people, five thousand years ago, had so much sense, what's happened to our sense? Because we are trying to live by their values and belief systems, that's why there is so much conflict.

The very existence is happening according to a pattern, and that is a subjective law. That is unchanging. This law may not be logically decoded. It can be perceived, but never articulated. We can only set up systems through which people can know it. Other realities keep changing, but the subjective law never changes. It is absolute. It is not connected to the physical, the psychological or genetic or social realities which are subject to change.

People are always trying to project the conflict on the planet as good versus evil; but it has never been so. It is always one man's belief versus another man's belief. Isn't it so? Why do you believe something first of all? We have always been trying to produce good human beings; that means somewhere you believe the Creator has done a bad job on creation. What we need is not good human beings; we need sensible human beings. Goodness is not what we need; we need sense on this planet right now, isn't it? We badly need sense. If you are sensible you wouldn't get into any trouble. If your sense is in full function, you will handle your life well; you will do what's best for yourself, isn't it?

'It's considered totally obscene to make any request to God, because if he doesn't know, what's the point asking him?'

Seeker: We saw this occult temple on the way to Kedarnath. Now, what is the purpose of creating such a temple and how does it benefit the pilgrims?

Sadhguru: The occult temple, the Bhairaveshwara temple,

on the way to Kedar, is not made for the sake of normal pilgrims who are going up the mountain. This is made for a particular type of people who are in a certain level of sadhana, a certain level of receptivity and mastery in their lives. It is for certain sadhakas who need assistance in certain dimensions.

See, in modern terms, let's say you are doing some work: you are making some product, manufacturing something, running an industry. Your customer is somewhere else, your supplier is somewhere else, but in between there is a consultant. So the occult temple plays the role of a consultant for people who are in certain levels of sadhana and who do not know what to do next, or who are stuck in certain situations within themselves. If they know how to access that temple, the energy could help them to go beyond that.

It is not a possibility for liberation. See, the consultant will not manufacture anything for you, will not produce anything for you. But still, consultants thrive in the world because that little assistance they give you here and there, makes a difference. So, in a way, the occult temple is a kind of consultant for sadhakas who are in certain types of sadhana – mainly people who are on the path of kriya, and who are doing intense processes to transform their energies, but for whom certain dimensions are knotted or tied up. That temple is not built for the normal pilgrim who is going just with his faith or belief.

That's why it's built in a small and insignificant way, so people need not attach too much importance to it, need not spend too much time with it. Probably, on that day, we were the only group of people who actually sat in the temple; most people wouldn't have even noticed that temple. So the temple is only for those who are in a certain level of knowing, not for a normal pilgrim.

Seeker: Can we go and worship at these occult temples?

Sadhguru: Occult temples are not really made for your normal kind of worship. Anyway, you need to understand the difference and distinction between worship and prayer. Maybe you just know prayer, you don't know any worship.

In the culture of Shiva, it's considered obscene to ask the Creator to do something as if he doesn't know what he should do. It's considered totally obscene to make any request to God, because if he doesn't know, what's the point asking him?

So worship is a certain elaborate system and a process to create certain inner situations within yourself. Worship in India involves elaborate procedures which entail a tremendous amount of mental application. It is a certain sadhana. It is a kind of kriya for a devotee. Action that you perform with your body, or your mind, or your emotion, is called karma. Action that is performed internally is called a kriya. So a worshipful attitude or a worshipful action is a kriya; it is an inner action performed with a devout attitude.

See, right now you are doing the morning kriya. We are not asking for devotion, because you are twenty-first century. (*Laughter*) Technically also, it'll work. When you come on the first day to the yoga program – very secular and logical and correct and educated – if I tell you, 'See, you must do this with devotion', you will leave, many of you. So we created kriyas which do not need any particular attitude; they just need focus, that's all. Right now the kriyas that you are doing are of that kind, which do not really require any kind of devotion. Just do it right, it'll work. It's very technical.

So worship, or what we refer to as pooja, is a kriya with devotion involved in it. It's a complex mixture of a certain technicality and emotion. Emotion and technology is a dangerous mix unless it is handled very properly, isn't it? If you handle any technology with emotion, it's dangerous. It is because of this that those people, who are handling technology and trying to free themselves of emotion, became like dry sticks. They are afraid; they know this much that if emotion comes into handling technology, it can be a disaster. They do not know how to keep their emotions away at a certain time, so they destroy the emotion in them. They will become so barren and almost inhuman in so many ways. But pooja or worship is this dangerous combination of technology and emotion.

So when we talk about occult temples, prayer is meaningless, because it's a technology – a subjective technology – that won't work without the right attitude. Occult is not spirituality. Occult is just technology. Like today, you can pick up your cell phone right now here, from Pipalkoti you can talk to somebody in the United States. This is technology. Occult is just like this: you can talk to somebody in the United States without the cell phone. It's a little more technology. That too will happen after some time as technology evolves.

Now, from that Graham Bell's instrument, it's come to this. A day will come when this is not necessary either. Already, you know, I have a Bluetooth mechanism where I don't have to dial. If I just say the person's name, it dials for me. If I say, 'Ashram', it'll go to the ashram number. A day will come where even this will not be needed. A small implant here (*points to the head*) will be enough. Whoever I want to talk to anywhere in the world, it will just happen.

So occult means that without the blue chip you still manage to talk. It's just technology on a different level, that's all. It is just purely technology; physical technology. I hesitate to use the word, 'subjective', but it is still subjective because you are not using any external objects. You are just using your body and mind and energy to do these things. Ultimately, no matter what technology, you're only using your body, mind and energy, isn't it? But you are picking up some external material and using it. Initially, if you wanted to manufacture a phone or an instrument you had to take a considerable amount of material. Now you are only taking a little material, and trying to reduce that further and further. So a day will come when we don't need any material; that'll be occult. Modern science and occult are bound to meet somewhere, if some small changes happen in our understanding of what's what.

So occult is purely technology, and this technology is becoming more and more irrelevant by the day because modern technology is advancing at a great pace. Now, to get to talk to somebody in the United States without the cell phone may take lots of preparation and effort. And even if you manage to contact them, they may say 'wrong number' (*Laughter*), because they don't recognize you. I know this from experience. (*Laughs*) So, occult is becoming more and more irrelevant. As modern technology becomes subtler and subtler, the need for occult will come down.

If you were doing the Char Dham Yatra by foot and there was no cell phone, and if you are gone for two years from your family, then occult would have been extremely important, isn't it? Just so that you could tell your family, 'I am okay, I am in Pipalkoti.' Yes? It would have been tremendously important. But today because we have the cell phone in our pocket, it is not so important to learn how to contact your family without the phone. Today we have an instrument which everybody, even a child, can use. So occult becomes more and more irrelevant as technology progresses.

So don't waste your time in occult temples.

But there are certain other dimensions to occult which could be used as a stepping stone to a spiritual process, because in many ways occult is the final step of physicality. The subtlest point of physicality is what we are using. See, the physical can be used in many ways. For example, if you take information technology, what started as a stone tablet has now come to a tiny blue chip. What would take a whole mountain to be carved upon, today is encoded in a tiny chip. The physical has become subtler and subtler. So the subtlest dimension of the physical, when you use it, we call it occult. Occult is using the subtlest phenomenon of the physical, but it is still physical. Because it's the last step in physicality, it can also be used as a stepping-stone to go beyond the physical. So there are a variety of mantras and practices, different types of worship and different ways to bring forth forces and forms which are very powerful.

Do you know something about Purusha-Prakriti? You know what it means? Purusha means — if you want to put it in one way — masculine. Prakriti means feminine. So in trying to explain the creation the way it is, that which is the seed of creation, is called Purusha; it's male but it doesn't have an active role in life. It is just like human birth. The masculine just plants the seed, but the rest of the creation is all-feminine, isn't it? So the Mother Goddess, or Parvati or Kali, is held as Prakriti. She is the whole creation, but the seed for this creation is Shiva or Purusha. This can be explained as Shiva-Shakti or Purusha-Prakriti, yin and yang, and in so many ways.

We are not talking about just two aspects of creation; we are talking about creation and the source of creation. So the whole creation is referred to as feminine, and the source of creation is referred to as masculine. Shiva is inert. Very rarely he comes into activity; the rest of the time he is just inert. He is in meditation, he never moves. When he comes alive, he moves in exuberant ways, but otherwise he's inert. But Prakriti, or Parvati, or the Mother Goddess, is always active. The trees are growing, the dogs are barking, the flowers are blooming, human beings are being born – this is all Prakriti. This is all the work of the Mother. That's the way the creation is happening. You must understand, the fundamental forces in the existence are just personified. These are not to be seen as people.

So this whole process of occult is concerned with Prakriti, nothing to do with Shiva. Shiva is not concerned with occult, though he is a master of occult. People who practice occult never worship Shiva. They worship Shiva from a distance, but their daily worship is only for the Devi or different forms of the Mother Goddess. These forms can be created. This has been there everywhere in the world, but in this land, they actively created a variety of feminine forms which are very powerful.

For example, Kali. Kali is not just an idol. Many yogis and

mystics worked to create a certain energy form which functions in a certain way and responds to a certain name. Usually they created very fierce forms because, for one, these are fierce people who cannot live with a tame woman. They want somebody really wild, so they created really wild women, and these are energy forms which are still alive and which respond to a particular mantra. When they created this form, a particular sound was associated with it. So one who uses that particular sound or mantra in a particular way can bring forth that form. Using this subtle form of energy, many things can be done. This is what the whole science of occult is about. Certain occult temples are created for a certain form, and you can call forth that form and do a variety of things.

I think these kinds of things have been talked about in a different way in other cultures. They believed that someday if you find a lamp and if you rub it, a genie will come. (*Laughter*) Yes? So occult forms were created like this and even today people can bring them down and do a variety of things. The whole system of Tantra is based on this. You've heard of Aghoris? Shiva is an Aghori. The Aghori form of yoga is very much oriented toward this.

There is a huge culture of Devi worship in India. Not only in India, but in Arabia, Europe, everywhere. Goddess worship was the most prominent thing till these monotheistic religions came up. All the Crusades and Inquisitions were mainly against people who were Goddess worshippers. Are you aware of this? After Islam came to Arabia, they went against all Goddess worship and went about burning up all the temples (because in Arabia the temples were wooden). And in Europe they did the same thing. They just tried to completely banish the feminine from the planet. But in India, she lived and she continues to live. Everywhere else, wherever the monotheistic religions dominated, they completely erased feminine worship.

One crucial point held against these Devi-worshipping or Goddess-worshipping groups was that they were doing Devil's work. That's because they were doing things that other people could not grasp or understand. They could do things that others would not have the means to do. That means they were into occult. Because they could perform occult, they were branded Devil worshippers and put to death, or their places of worship burnt, and systematically over centuries, they were completely erased. I think it's totally absent in Europe, except among a few gypsy tribes which have kept it alive even today. They are nomads, who don't stay in one place, because they were afraid of persecution.

Here it's still a very strong culture. But today, even here people conduct the Devi worship in a clandestine way because of social pressures. People have become educated. Anything that doesn't appeal to their reason, they want to destroy, you know. Because of this, most of the Devi temples conduct the core of their worship in secret, not known to the outside world, just to a small group of people. Everybody is never involved in this, because unfortunately society has become so male-dominated.

When I say male-dominated, I don't mean man is dominating. That's not true. (*Laughter*) I mean, the male mind is dominating. Woman also has become a man today. That's the most unfortunate thing. Women think they are becoming free by becoming like men. This is the most horrible slavery – that a woman has to become like a man. The logical mind, the masculine mind, is dominating the world. Once the masculine mind dominates the world, anything that doesn't appeal to reason will be destroyed. This is happening worldwide. Here also it's happening, but you can't kill it totally because it's too deep-rooted. There are still some hardcore people like me – people who have still kept the feminine alive in them. There are many of them and they will keep it alive. But I think this feminine worship will never be mainstream anywhere in the world. It'll always be clandestine.

'Every moment of your life, what the trees exhale, you inhale; what you exhale, they inhale. This is a constant transaction, a constant partnership... that nobody can break...'

Seeker: The amount of pollution I saw on this journey was unbelievable. Isn't there something people can do to address this?

Sadhguru: The question is always about who is going to stop it, because all of us want all the comforts. Everybody, everywhere — not just you — wants all the comforts. And one of the comforts that we have is plastic bags. A paper bag, a cloth bag, is cumbersome; a plastic bag is so comfortable, you know? But over a period of time, when a pile of stuff gathers, then we start thinking about the problem that it creates.

Now you are talking about yourself — people who come from a certain educated background, who have a certain awareness about environment. But the simple pilgrim who is coming from the village, he doesn't know all this. He doesn't believe that throwing the plastic bag is going to do something to such a big mountain. He doesn't think so; I want you to understand that. The simple villager, who comes from somewhere, does not even understand that throwing a plastic bag is going to affect such a big mountain; he'll laugh at you. If you tell him throwing a plastic bag is going to affect the Himalayas, he will laugh because it's such a big mountain: 'What, a plastic bag will affect it?' So awareness has to be brought forth, which doesn't happen overnight. And anyway, if one day they make up their minds, you know in a week or ten days' time, it would all be cleaned up. So the plastic bag is not the great environmental issue right now.

The real environmental issue is global warming, which is threatening Kedar in a big way. Glaciers are melting much more rapidly than ever before, which could threaten the temple itself. The lakes are filling up on the top. If they break forth from there, that could be really disastrous.

So if we are really concerned about it, that's what we need to look at. Every time we turn on the air conditioner, turn on our cars, we need to be a little more aware of it. We can't stop it; our lives are like that. But just being a little more aware about it, could help. A poor villager comes and throws a plastic bag; that's not the main issue now. The issue is with the affluent, isn't it?

Seeker: But what can the affluent do? What can we do?

Sadhguru: For the last twenty-six to twenty-seven years, almost every year I have been in the Himalayas for a short period of time and I know these mountains so well, every peak. I have never seen the peaks that I am talking about not clad in snow. They have always have been snow-clad, any season of the year. But now I am deeply distressed to see that lots of these peaks are completely bare. Completely bare, for the first time. This is not a joke. This is a recipe for disaster. This is not a prediction; this is a simple calculation. If you perform certain actions, certain consequences will naturally come your way. And they are coming our way. It looks like we are living here as if we are the last generation on this planet, which is very distressing.

The next generation of people, our children, if they look

back at us, they will look back at us with great animosity, because we are leaving behind a land which is no good for anything. If you leave the country and the world in such a disastrous state, definitely our children will suffer. How we take care of our planet will decide the quality of life that they will have in the future.

As we find economic well-being, which is going to happen in a big way in the next ten years for various reasons, it's extremely important we take concrete ecological steps — holding back carbon emission and whatever else that is leading to very drastic climate changes in the world. So one simple thing that we can do is increase the green coverage on the planet by planting trees. That is the simplest thing that we can do.

Biologically, they've told you that trees are not like you, they don't bleed like you, so they are not related to you. See, you may not be on talking terms with your own friends, your family, your parents, your wife, your husband, your children. Off and on you transact with them. But every moment of your life, what the trees exhale, you inhale; what you exhale, they inhale. This is a constant transaction, a constant partnership, a constant relationship that nobody can break, that nobody can afford to live without. So our closest relative is plant life. Our closest relatives are trees and if we grow trees, they will grow us. They have definitely been nurturing us always. We forgot this and our sufferings have multiplied.

I will promise you this — and this may sound a little presumptuous for people who come from the medical profession — that if you bring thirty per cent green coverage in Tamil Nadu, a minimum of fifteen to twenty per cent of chronic ailments will go down in the state for sure. Just like what you breathe has become poison, what you eat is becoming poison, what you drink is becoming poison slowly... Where is the question of health? Where is the question of well-being?

This whole process of launching 'Project Green Hands' and planting trees — we have been doing this for over ten to fifteen years — is fundamentally to increase this awareness right across the state, so that educated or uneducated, rich or poor, capable or incapable, everybody is willing to plant one tree. This is about inspiring people to make something happen which is so very fundamental to our well-being.

'Once you have an inkling of the immensity of life, once you see how small and stupid you are, you become receptivity itself.'

Seeker: This may sound like a strange question. But how can we conserve the energies we receive from the Himalayas and from you?

Sadhguru: What are the methods to preserve whatever you obtained, either from the Himalayas or from anywhere?

See, the kriyas that have been taught to you are very foundational. In the twenty-five or thirty minutes that you spend on kriyas, there is no exuberant experience, usually. They are not designed to give you an exuberant experience because they are just there to build your life, block by block, brick by brick. There are other kinds of practices which we could teach you, where in ten minutes, you will be in exuberant states of experience, but they are not this foundational.

When I say 'foundational', it means that if you give yourself to it, you are changing the very fundamentals of your life, very slowly, just block by block. No drama, no great changes all of a sudden, nothing that you cannot handle. But if you look at who you were one year ago and who you are today, there's a huge difference. You never noticed when all this happened. That's how it should happen. If sudden changes happen, most of you cannot handle it. So the kriyas that you are practicing are an excellent method. To preserve whatever you want to preserve, you need a good foundation, isn't it? If you don't have a good foundation, you'll play around like that for two days and again collapse to the same old state. If you want to get somewhere, it's very important that you build a solid foundation. An energy foundation for yourself is necessary if something has to be built on top of it which is enduring, which will take you through life and death. If you just want fanciful experiences today, we can create them very easily, but they may not endure.

So the sadhana that you are doing is more than enough. There is no need to bring more and more practices into life. The same practice can be raised into different dimensions of experience and practice.

Seeker: Apart from doing our practices and having faith in you, is there anything else we can do to increase our receptivity?

Sadhguru: If you just don't make your thoughts, emotions, opinions, ideas, beliefs and yourself, important, you are absolutely receptive. The only barrier is yourself, nothing else. You just keep your ideas, opinions, thoughts, emotions, aside. Just see them as stupid.

The moment you think you know what is good for you, your ability to receive is crippled. Only if you're hungry can you eat well. If you're full of things that you value, you cannot receive much. Only when you have no clue about the immensity of life, you think you are smart. When you see that the way you think and feel is not enough, you become receptive. Once you have an inkling of the immensity of life, once you see how small and stupid you are, you become receptivity itself.

'If you continue your sadhana you will find love is no more an emotion; it's just a certain way that you are.'

Seeker: Then what about love for the guru?

Sadhguru: Love for the guru? What about that?

Seeker: It's an emotion many of us experience.

Sadhguru: Hmm? It's quite stupid. (*Laughter*) Now, you need to understand, whomever you love – the guru, or the mountains, or your husband, or your children, or whatever – it's all your nonsense, isn't it? Yes or no? See, does the quality of your husband reflect in your love? Does the quality of your children reflect in your love? Does the quality of the mountains reflect in your love? Does the quality of the guru reflect in your love? It is just your emotion. It is not right; it is not wrong. Right now that is the most intense thing you know in your life, so intensify it. But it's quite a stupid thing. Because you don't know any better, that's what you do.

When I say 'stupid,' I am not saying, destroy it. You cannot destroy it. Within you, the most pleasant situation within you is when you're in love, isn't it? When you have some feeling for love, that's the most pleasant way of existence you know about yourself. It's not everything. People are always talking about divine love. See, love is a human emotion. It is the most pleasant way to be. You can say it's the most wonderful way for you to exist. But is it the ultimate way? No. Love means, fundamentally, you are still longing to become one with something or somebody. So you are just longing. It never delivers you there; it is just a vehicle. It is not the destination. Love is not the destination;

love is just a vehicle which takes you in a certain direction.

Now, you want to become one. This emotion makes you feel almost like you are one, but never really makes you one, isn't it? So at some point you get sufficiently frustrated with your love, when it is taking you but not delivering you anywhere. Maybe you felt like that when they were driving the bus. You know, it looks like they are not going anywhere. It looks like the whole thing is about the bus ride. So if it doesn't deliver you anywhere, then after some time this bus will become frustrating. Initially, it will be fun. After some time it does become frustrating, isn't it? Because after some time you want to go somewhere. You want to become one with something.

So when you say 'love for the guru', it doesn't matter what the object of your love is: whether you love the mountains, or the guru, or the temple, or your mother, or your father. That's not the point. The point is if you make yourself into an atmosphere of love, the possibility of going through this world more pleasantly is definitely there for you, no matter what's happening around you. So especially if you want to walk the spiritual path, keeping yourself – your interiority – pleasant, is extremely important because it's a very challenging path. If you know how to keep your interiority pleasant, if your emotions are pleasant always, then walking the path becomes a joyful process.

If you are not like this, if there's no love in you, then you must know something else. You must know the blissfulness of just your existence: not being happy *about* something; just being blissful, your very existence being blissful. Every cell in your body has become sweet. You don't love anybody, you don't like anybody or dislike anybody – you are just pleasant. When you are simply so sweet and pleasant within yourself, your very presence is pleasant. You don't have to kick up an emotion to be pleasant. Anything that you look at, anything that you touch or don't touch – everything is experienced as sweetness. Until you are like this, it's good to be in love, the best way to be.

But why so much importance has been laid upon love for the guru is because of a certain misunderstanding and a certain understanding. Now the moment you love somebody, you expect that somebody to respond to you. When that somebody responds, a certain transaction happens between two people. And after some time this transaction leads to certain sense of expectation and bondage. A certain type of behavior is expected; a certain way of living is expected. Otherwise it causes immense pain to one or the other. It keeps happening. The reason why they talked about love for the guru is because he is playing the game just to the extent that you must fall in love with him, but at the same time he will never get entangled with you. You can get entangled with him as much as you want. There's no danger of him holding you up.

So you will go through a certain phase of deep

entanglement; it's okay. But slowly, if you continue your sadhana you will find, love is no more an emotion; it's just a certain way that you are. Now it's not emotion. Your energies just reverberate with him. It is no more emotional. From an emotional state, we can gradually shift it to an energy state. Your connection with him is simply energetic, and that's very good. That's a wonderful way to be, because in that state, the ultimate possibility is so close. In that state, a guru has so much more freedom to do what he wants to do with you. But right now, emotion is an important part of you, directing you in some direction. Without emotion, you can't be involved. That's the way you are made right now, isn't it? So emotion is okay; nothing wrong with it.

'Compassion is definitely a more liberating emotion than love.'

Seeker: Since we're on the subject of love, what is the difference between love and compassion?

Sadhguru: Out of all the emotions that you can nurture within you, compassion is the least entangling, and at the same time, the most liberating emotion that you can have. You can live without compassion also. But anyway, you have emotions. It's better to turn your emotions into compassion rather than anything else, because every other emotion has the capability of getting entangled. Compassion is one dimension of emotion which is liberating, which doesn't get entangled with anything or anybody.

Generally, your love is fueled by passion. Compassion means it's an all-encompassing passion. When it is exclusive, we call it passion. When it becomes all-inclusive, it becomes compassion. 'Love' initially starts with a certain liking, so it is dependent upon somebody or something being good – to you, of course. So you are always counting on the goodness of something or somebody. Or in other words, that emotion gets limited. Only if the person whom you love is good, you can continue to love them. If they turn out to be whatever you think is bad, then you cannot love them.

But the advantage of compassion is if somebody is very bad, in a pathetic condition, in an evil mood, you can have more compassion for him. So compassion is a liberating emotion that way. It is not limiting you. It is not making a distinction between good and bad. So compassion is definitely a more liberating emotion than love.

Love is always, generally at least, about somebody. It is exclusive. It can be beautiful, but it's very exclusive. If two lovers sit together, the rest of the world is excluded from them; they have created their own artificial world of togetherness. Basically, it's like a conspiracy. You always enjoy your conspiracy, because in conspiracy you become special; nobody else knows about it. Usually for most people, the joy of love is just this: that it's a conspiracy. They fall in love, they enjoy it very much, but when they get married, it's declared to the world. And suddenly all the fancy stuff goes out of it, because it's no more a conspiracy. Everybody knows about it.

So there is a conspiracy angle to love which brings lots of pressure for people. But in the very exclusiveness, in the very nature of excluding the rest of the world, suffering can be brought about. Suffering will be brought about if you exclude existence from your experience. If it starts as a passion and expands into unbounded compassion, that's fine. But if it starts as passion and ends as passion, you're asking for lots of trouble in your life. So one is entangling; another is liberating.

Part Three

No Take-away
Badrinath

'A little insufficiency has brought you here;
utter insufficiency will deliver you.'

According to the Skanda Purana: 'There are several sacred shrines in heaven, on earth, and in hell; but there is no shrine like Badrinath.'

Extolled as the holiest of holy places in scriptures and legends for thousands of years, Badrinath evokes a welter of associations for the Indian pilgrim — with Nara and Narayana, with Vishnu and Shiva, with Adi Shankara and Sage Vyasa, with the Pandavas and the river goddess Ganga, among a host of others.

Sadhguru sheds light on this great site of Indian pilgrimage, situated in the rolling hills of Garhwal, along the banks of the river Alaknanda. He tells the legend of the wily coup by which Vishnu ousted Shiva from his rightful habitat. He tells of Adi Shankara, mystic philosopher of the ninth century, who discovered the black stone image of Lord Badrinarayan (later enshrined in the temple), and established this as a major pilgrimage spot. He talks of his own indescribable experience at Kanti Sarovar, near Kedarnath, in which the entire universe manifested itself to him as sound.

The chapter also offers fascinating insights on the seemingly inscrutable ways of spiritual masters and sadhus, as it addresses varied questions: Why do some spiritual practitioners interact with people and others keep their distance? Why are those who walk the spiritual path always scrutinized and judged by society? Do disciples choose gurus, or the other way around?

And running through the chapter like a recurrent motif is Sadhguru's reminder, a brutally, uncomfortably succinct reminder: 'Stop the take-away business. Simply be.'

'How Shiva and Parvati became illegal aliens…'

You know the story behind Badrinath? It's like this. This is where Shiva and Parvati lived. It was their home. One day Narada went to Narayana or Vishnu and said, 'You are a bad example for humanity. All the time you are just lying around on Adishesha, and your wife, Lakshmi, is constantly serving you and spoiling you silly. You are not a good example for other creatures on the planet. For all the other beings in the creation, you must do something more purposeful.'

So to escape this criticism and also work for his own uplift – you know even gods have to do it – Vishnu came down to the Himalayas looking for the right kind of place to do his austerities and his sadhana. Then he found Badrinath, a nice little home, with everything just the way he thought it should be, an ideal place for his sadhana. So he went into the house. Then he realized, this is Shiva's abode – and that man is dangerous. If he gets angry, he is the kind who can cut off his own throat, not just yours. The man is very dangerous.

So Narayana transformed himself into a little child and sat in front of the house. Shiva and Parvati, who had gone out for a walk, returned home. Narayana was crying his heart out as a baby. Parvati's feminine compassion was aroused; she went and tried to grab the child. Shiva stopped her and said, 'Don't touch that child.'

Parvati said, 'How cruel. What nonsense are you talking? I am going to pick up this child. See how the child is crying.'

Shiva said, 'Don't believe whatever you see. I am telling you, don't pick up the child.'

But Parvati's feminine emotions for the child had overtaken her, and she said, 'No, it doesn't matter what you say. The mother in me will not allow me to let the child be like this. I am going to take the child.'

Shiva said, 'This is not a child; don't take it.'

But Parvati said, 'Nothing doing,' and grabbed the child and put it on her lap. The child was very comfortable on her lap, and sat there very gleefully looking at Shiva.

Shiva knew the consequence of this, but what to do? So he said, 'Okay, let's see what happens.'

Then Parvati comforted and fed the child, left him at home and went with Shiva for a hot water bath. You know the hot water pool in Badri? Same pool. So they went for a bath. Then they came back to the house and found the doors were locked from inside. Then Shiva knew, okay, the game has started.

Parvati was aghast. 'Who has closed the door?'

Shiva said, 'I told you, don't pick up this child. You brought the child into the house, now he has locked the door.'

Parvati said, 'What shall we do?'

Shiva had two options: one was to burn up everything in front of him; another was just to find another way and go. So he said, 'Let's go somewhere else. Because it's your beloved baby, I cannot touch it. (*Laughs*) I cannot do anything about it now. Let's go somewhere else.'

So that is how Shiva and Parvati became illegal aliens. Is that the term? (*Laughs*) Suddenly, with a new refugee status, they started walking. Actually, between Badrinath and Kedarnath, it is only a ten kilometer distance from peak to peak. So they slowly walked around, looking for an ideal place to live. They finally settled down in Kedar. And this is how Shiva lost his own home. 'Did he not *know*?' you may ask. You know many things, but you still allow them to happen.

'That's been the intention of our work also: not to establish a new religion, or a new scripture, but to establish the spiritual sciences just as a way of life...'

Historically also, Badrinath has a certain significance, because the temple here was installed by Adi Shankara. Adi Shankara, for those of you who do not know, was born in Kerala around the ninth century. He was born in a place called Kaladi in Kerala, about two hundred kilometers down south of Coimbatore. And he walked up and down the country three times. East to west he walked once, north to south he walked three times. And in his short span of thirty-two years of life, he did incredible things. At the age of two, he could fluently speak and write Sanskrit. At the age of eight, he knew all the four Vedas inside out. So he was an extraordinary scholar with almost superhuman capabilities.

In these thirty-two years of life, the things that he has done are simply, humanly, quite impossible. If you have to walk up and down, along the mountains — it's something like 3,200 to 3,400 kilometers north to south — you can imagine what it must mean. Tomorrow when you are riding on the bus, you will wonder how anybody could have walked through this. But he walked up and down three times. Once when he was up in the north, he came to know his mother was dying, and he walked all the way down to Kerala. He spent a few days with his mother until she died and again went back.

Within these twenty-four years of his life — from age eight to thirty-two — he produced works that were masterpieces for which there is no comparison anywhere. Even today, in terms of scholarship there is nothing like his *Soundarya Lahari* in the Sanskrit language. Nobody knows where, in the middle of all this walking up and down the land, he got the time to write. (*Laughs*)

His guidance was from his guru, Gowdapada. Gowdapada is very much a part of our tradition also. His teachings are very much a part of Isha in so many ways. Gowdapada was an extraordinary guru, but his teachings were never written down. He made sure it was not written down. He must have taught thousands of people but he produced fifteen to twenty good people who re-established the spiritual science in the country. Very quietly, without any noise, without starting a new religion or anything, he did this. In many ways, that's been the intention of our work also: not to establish a new religion, or a new scripture, but to establish the spiritual sciences just as a way of life, just as an inculcation within a human being. So Gowdapada was a very, very different kind altogether. With his guidance, Shankara went about doing all this incredible work.

Shankara was brought up in the Brahmin culture, so he thought in some ways as a Brahmin still. One day towards the end of his life, he had his bath and was about to enter the temple. Then somebody who maintained the graveyard – you know, he is considered the lowest of the low castes – came his way. I know an undertaker is not so bad in western countries, (Laughs) but in India someone who takes care of the shmashaan or graveyard was seen as the lowest of the low. So, that man came his way.

Shankara said, 'I was just about to go into the temple and you came in my path and spoiled my day. Move away.'

Now that lowly man was a realized being. He said, 'Who
should move? Me or my body?'

That question struck Shankara. And that's it. All his
teaching came before that. After that, he never gave any
teaching. He walked away to Kedar and he disappeared. At
the age of thirty-two, he left. Even today there is a
monument for him. You will see just his hand and staff
carved in marble. Out of a wall, a hand and staff are jutting
out. He disappeared there. Nobody knows where he went.

So this temple was installed by Adi Shankara. It's a visually
incredible place.

'The most sought-after objects have come my way of their
own accord.'

Seeker: You've traveled these mountains innumerable times
– frequently on your own – and we hear you've had some
strange experiences. I heard you once met a sadhu who gave
you a rare rudraksha*. Could you tell us more?

Sadhguru: In September 1993, I landed in Hardwar, not
knowing where I should go. I soon started off towards
Badrinath. Sixteen hours of bus ride, snaking through the
mountains, were most memorable, almost like finding my
way back into the womb. Even now I know almost every
curve on that road.

---

*sacred beads, seeds of a tree found mostly in the Himalayas, also known to have
many medicinal and spiritual qualities

I reached Badri at 7 pm. It was dark and cold. I had absolutely no warm clothes. I was in my jeans, T-shirt and my shoes. I managed to find a shelter. It was beginning to snow.

Next morning – it must have been 5.30 – I came out for a cup of tea. It looked like that was the only refuge from cold, as the bedclothes that were provided were wet. It was still dark and very cold. I braced myself and walked on finding my way to the chai shop. The room key that I held in my hand, which was numb with cold, slipped and fell on the ground.

I bent down to pick it up. And as I looked up, what I saw is something even the craftiest bard would fail to describe. I was in a valley that was pitch-dark but the snow-clad mountain peak was brightly lit. It was pure white with the golden sun. It completely overpowered me. All that I had heard, read, seen and imagined fell woefully short of what was there before me. Tears were my only answer. Then I knew these were tears of reunion.

I was so enchanted with the whole place that it never occurred to me to visit the temple. I just walked towards Vasudhara, a waterfall – a twelve kilometer walk. Many sadhus I met on the way welcomed me as 'Maharaj'. I had no inclination to respond, so I kept walking. Vasudhara is a four-hundred-foot-high waterfall. Just a thin wisp – most of it just gets lost in the wind. Very little reaches the ground

below. I sat on a rock a little distance away, where only a
faint spray could reach me.

I closed my eyes, as I always see better that way. I suddenly
felt someone holding my feet, crying and pleading, 'Maharaj'.
I opened my eyes and saw a sadhu. He spoke in a language
other than Hindi, but whatever he said was clear to me. He
was appealing to me, saying that only I could pull him out
of his spiritual stagnation.

I then initiated him into Shoonya* dhyana. Generally, I can
barely speak Hindi, but I spoke fluent Hindi then. I said,
'Parvat jaise atal raho.' (Be still like these mountains). The
sadhu settled into a deep shoonya state, with tears streaming
down his cheeks.

Then as a token of his gratitude he offered me an
'ekamukhi'** rudraksha, the size of a large lemon. When I
took it in my hands, it was thumping with energy. When I
placed it in my pocket, it was thumping like an excited heart.
I returned to my room after that with the rarest of rare
rudrakshas in my possession.

Next year again the urge to go to the Himalayas was strong,
and I went there twice in the same year. Again I travelled

---

*a meditation process of conscious and effortless non-doing

**a one-faced rudraksha, considered to be the rarest and most powerful of all
rudraksha beads, representative of Lord Shiva and used by people of the highest
spiritual attainments

alone. In the train, I remember a family in the compartment. They made many attempts to strike a conversation with me, but I did not respond. Those two-and-a-half days in the train, I mostly had my eyes closed. I was there as if I was alone, not even recognizing their presence, perhaps to the point of rudeness. This family of three was to disembark at Agra. I once noticed the lady looking at me and crying. I'm sure she herself did not know why.

I reached Hardwar with no particular schedule or plan. But something in me just took me towards Kedarnath. I reached Gowrikund around 3 p.m., but decided to trek fourteen kilometers to Kedarnath. It started raining, with temperatures on the minus side. Chilled to my bones, I made this climb of fourteen kilometers. I reached Kedar around 8 p.m. and went a little further to reach a small ashram located close to the snow-clad peaks, at a beautiful meadow beside a small brook that flowed along, making a chuckling noise. During the day I travelled down to Kedar and spent the day with sadhus of various sects like Nagas, Kanphats, and others. These are ascetics who normally keep aloof, but they were very close to me and very excited. One of them belonged to Salem and has visited Velliangiri. He was simply overwhelmed.

When I later went to the Shiva temple at Guptakashi, it was as if the place, the temple and the priests were all known to me and I had been to this place before. Many sadhus recognized me and fell at my feet, but I did not reveal my identity. Nor did I want to communicate with them. One beautiful thing about Himalayas is that there are many people there who recognize you for what you are. Even when I was traveling by bus, many sadhus turned around and gave me a smile or nod of recognition. It is a homecoming. It is these sadhus and sanyasins who make the place more alluring than the mountains.

From here I moved to a small town on the Indo-Nepalese border where all the rudraksha beads from Nepal generally reach. One sadhu here gave me a rare 'shankh' – a three-in-one conch shell – which signifies prosperity. Even though there was no real need for me to have it, he just left it with me and walked away. The most sought-after objects have come my way of their own accord.

'In yoga, we say the whole of existence is sound.'

Seeker: At Kedar, you mentioned the 'Nada Brahma' song and how it suddenly came to you. Could you say something more about that experience?

Sadhguru: 'Nada Brahma' simply means experiencing the world as a sound, not as a form. We know through modern science also that every sound has a form attached to it, and every form has a sound attached to it. This is a scientific reality. And today we also know that the whole existence is just a vibration of energies. There is no such thing as matter any more, as far as science is concerned. So where there is a vibration, there is bound to be a sound. So in yoga, we say the whole of existence is sound.

This happened eight or nine years ago. I used to travel every year alone for a month or two in the Himalayas by myself. You know what it means to get into the GMOU bus? Every second or third bus that comes in front of you is marked 'GMOU Limited.' You didn't see that? The GMOU bus leaves Hardwar at 3.30 or 3.45 in the morning, reaches Badrinath by about 7-7.30 in the evening. It has to pass this 3 o'clock gate, so we were trying to race against time. We were just racing from Rampur, which is less than half the way. Our driver and everybody on the bus was in anxiety over whether we'll cross in time or not.

These buses are called 'Bhookh Hartaal'. (*Laughter*) That means it's a hunger-strike bus. If you get into it, the driver will stop for neither food nor toilet. In the morning if you get in, till the evening he will drive like a madman, not stopping anywhere. (*Laughter*) So people with small bladders should not get into these buses (*Laughs*); it will just go on and on and on. And he will only stop in between to drop and pick up passengers. And the driver has got his own chapati rolls, which he keeps eating as he drives. If you want to get yours, when he just stops somewhere, you run to the nearest shop, pick up two chapatis with bhaji over them, come running back and eat it. Otherwise, if you don't have that kind of wherewithal, you just sit there hungry.

So I was traveling by those GMOU buses. I couldn't bear
to sit in those buses because of the stink and all the hassles.
So I somehow took permission and always managed to sit
on the top. I just covered my nose with a handkerchief or a
towel, tied it just to bear the stink, wore glasses and sat
there on top of the bus throughout. So I land up in Kedar
like this, at probably 6.45–7 in the evening, and I just go
right up. With just one thin T-shirt and a little thicker T-
shirt, one over the other, no warm clothes, I started climbing
Kedar in the night. It was drizzling. By the time you reach
there early in the morning, you're all wet. (Those days I
was made in a different way!) I climbed there and I spent
some time in Kedar. I don't know if you noticed this: to
the left of the temple was a little climbing road, and there
was a huge rock and a few flags hoisted there. That's a little
ashram which I was supposed to inherit. (*Laughs*)

There was one Ananda Margi, who had dropped out of the
Ananda Marga* path. You know what Ananda Marga is?
You might have seen these posters and stickers stuck
everywhere; nobody knows who stuck them and what it
meant, but always it said, 'PROUT* for Prosperity.' Have
you seen this slogan? At one time in India in the '70s,
everywhere you looked, you saw these posters. Nobody

---

*Ananda Marga or the Path of Bliss was founded by Prabhat Ranjan Sarkar (Shri
    Shri Anandamurti) in 1955 in the town of Jamalpur in the state of Bihar. He
taught spiritual practices for self development and urged aspirants to take a strong
                                    stand against exploitation and corruption.
*The Progressive Utilisation Theory (PROUT), propounded in 1959, was a socio-
                    economic theory, based on the values of neo-humanism.

knew who was writing this all over the country, but everywhere there used to be this slogan. So this was an Ananda Margi — retired or dropped out. And now he is called Phalahari Baba because he eats only dried nuts and fruits and cooked potatoes.

So I went there because, you know, I want to stay in that kind of atmosphere and I also have very little money in my pocket. (*Laughs*) So I went and stayed with him. He gives me two slices of dried apple in the morning and that's it. There's no lunch in the ashram. Ashram means it's just two rooms attached to the big rock that you saw. There's a little stream, wonderful place; there's a meadow up there. And evening, he doesn't eat; he just gives me a little bit of cooked potato without any salt or anything. So you eat two potatoes in the evening, two slices of dried apple in the morning.

So I am on this diet for two days, and I am hungry. (*Laughter*) I am terribly hungry. I had heard about this place called Kanti Sarovar and one afternoon I decided to go there. I had had enough of this sage and these two slices of dried apple; I wanted to visit Shiva. I am sure he ate better. (*Laughter*) I decided to visit him.

So I set forth around 2.00–2.30 p.m. It was a sunny day. It was warm and I just wore my less thick T-shirt and went off. (*Laughs*) I think I got there in a little more than an hour's time. There was this lake and these snow-capped mountains. This time the snow is very low, and because it's not so cold, you probably enjoyed the place better. The last trip that we were here, it was at least cooler by about seven to eight degrees centigrade. The night temperatures were touching minus four, minus five; this time I think it didn't even touch zero in Kedar.

So I went up and sat there. In terms of nature, it's fantastic; there's no question about it. There's a huge lake. It's yet to become ice at that time; it's still water, but absolutely still. There's no vegetation, even though there's a lake. It's all snow-covered peaks reflecting in the totally still water. It's an incredible place.

I just sat there. The serenity, silence and purity penetrated my consciousness. The climb, the altitude, and the desolate beauty of that place left me breathless. I sat in that stillness on a small rock with my eyes open, imbibing every form around me. The surroundings gradually lost their form and only 'nada' – sound – existed. The mountain, the lake and the whole surrounding including my body did not exist in their usual form. Everything was just sound. Within me a song arose – 'Nada brahma vishwa swaroopa'.

I am somebody who always avoided learning the Sanskrit language. Though I liked that language very much and I knew the depth of the language, I avoided learning it because the moment you learn Sanskrit, you will invariably end up reading the scriptures. My own vision has never failed me in anything; not for one moment has it let me down. So I didn't want to clutter myself with scriptures and all these traditions. So I avoided the Sanskrit language.

I am sitting there; my mouth is definitely closed. My eyes are still open. And I hear this song in a big way, in my voice. It's my voice singing and it's a Sanskrit song. I hear it clearly, loudly. So loud it's like the whole mountain is singing. In my experience everything has turned into sound. That's when I perceived this song. I didn't make it up; I didn't write it. It just descended upon me. The whole song flowed out in Sanskrit. The experience was overpowering. Slowly, after some time, everything fell back into its earlier form. The fall of my consciousness — the fall from 'nada' to 'rupa' — filled my eyes with tears.

If you just give yourself to that song, there is a kind of power to it. It has a power to dissolve a person, if you really throw yourself into it. We could sing and wake up the whole town, but next time around we may not get accommodation here. (*Laughter*)

Tomorrow evening, we will be spending some time on the banks of the Ganga in Rishikesh. There will be a very beautiful little ritual on the banks of the river. An evening arati will happen for the river. That moment will be very ethereal and beautiful. The Ganga is not just a river for people; it's many more things. You may wonder: 'How can a river of water be sacred? What is all this nonsense?' But

if you are willing, anything can become sacred. Out of
people's willingness, they made the river sacred. 'Oh, that
means the river is not sacred; it's just what you believe?'
No. People can make anything sacred. Not just in their
minds; they can actually make anything sacred. That's how
it's been with this river, and especially certain parts of the
river.

I want you to experience tomorrow evening with utter
openness. Don't worry about the ritual, what your mind
says. Just give yourself to the process; at least enjoy it.
Visually, it's beautiful. Very very beautiful. That firelight,
that evening reflection in the river. You can all leave a lamp
in the water. It just floats away. It takes away all your sins
(*Laughter*) so that next year's sins can be accounted fresh.
It's a beautiful situation; I want you to experience and enjoy
this.

'If the guru is trying to fit into the disciples' expectations,
he is unfit to be a guru.'

Seeker: I recently met a sadhuni who was keeping a distance
from people and talking 'negative energy/ positive energy'
kind of stuff. And after she met some people, she would
go right away and wash her hands and face. I have always
loved the fact that you hug everybody and don't observe any
of these norms of purity and impurity. Is her behavior an
indication that she was not really that strong, spiritually?
Did she believe that someone could just suck your energy

away? Why was she so afraid of getting polluted by other people?

Sadhguru: Why are you asking me to make comments about somebody that I have not even met? I don't wish to talk about that person. But many sadhus wouldn't like to touch people — not because they think people are impure, not because of any other kind of prejudices. It is just that when they are in a certain level of sadhana, they want to establish their own energies in a certain way. So they don't want to get involved with people. For example, for our brahmacharis, we tell them not even to mix and wash their clothes with others'. Their clothes are always kept separately; their bedclothes are separate; everything is separate. That's because their whole work is about trying to establish their own stable energy. They don't want any kind of mix-up. So somebody who is in a certain sadhana may not want to touch people. I don't see why everybody should touch everybody. It's not necessary. If she doesn't feel like it, if she doesn't want to touch anybody, that's fine. And there is no need for you to make a judgment.

Somebody washing their hands when they touch somebody could be interpreted as some prejudice, that there is some impurity about people. But when somebody is in a certain state of sadhana, yes, he wouldn't like to be in any kind of physical contact with others. That's not because of any prejudice; that's because of a certain understanding. So somebody doesn't want to touch you. You don't have to be prejudiced against them; it's perfectly okay. They don't want to touch you; that's all there is. It is not necessary for people to think, if someone is evolved enough they have to touch you. It's not necessary. When I am in certain ways, even I don't like to be in contact with people; I would like to be alone by myself.

Seeker: Can you elaborate on that?

Sadhguru: When you are doing certain types of work, where you have made your energies much more malleable or fluid than normal, you also do it by creating a certain insulation. But when you are doing this in order to do a certain kind of work apart from the people around you, your energies are so fluid [that] you won't like to be in touch with other people because it could affect you in so many ways. There have been situations like this for me, where just in a certain moment, being in contact with people, not necessarily physically, I have – not intentionally, but at the same time, not totally helplessly – imbibed or taken away their diseases. And those diseases have manifested inside of my body, and are actually manifesting in my body. Such things have happened to me. And I know at those times I should have kept away from them. But at the same time, because of their need, their suffering, you reach out to them. It can happen.

That is not the only factor. Above all, it could disturb the work that you are doing. So during certain periods or certain times, we don't wish to be in touch. Especially a sadhaka, who is in a certain stage of sadhana, it's best for him to keep physically aloof from other people. So whatever this sadhuni is doing, maybe it's out of her wisdom that she is doing it, not out of her prejudice.

Seeker: Sadhguru, why is it that people on the spiritual path are always judged and analyzed by people? For example, though you are a master, you throw yourself into every activity with total zest. Like the other day in Rishi Valley, you were blowing bubbles with the children. In comparison, most other swamis are rather sober. So do you get judged more because of your relatively uninhibited behavior? And I also would like to know: is it the disciple who chooses the master or the master who chooses the disciple?

Sadhguru: That's too many things in one question!

About people making judgments about the spiritual, I want you to understand, this is not just about the spiritual people; they are doing this about everybody. That's one of their prime time jobs — analyzing and judging the whole world for what it is. It is just that analyzing a spiritual person is a lot more entertainment than analyzing somebody else. Because analyzing somebody else, you can easily draw conclusions. With a spiritual person, there is so much intrigue, so much mystery, that it becomes a very entertaining process for people to go on analyzing.

You talked about me being able to throw myself into any

activity – either throwing a stone into the river or blowing bubbles with kids, or anything for that matter. People have always tried to have a set idea about how a spiritual person should be, what kind of clothes he should wear, how he should speak, how he should be. They've got it all set. It's because of this set idea that every time an enlightened being comes along, he is persecuted because he doesn't happen to be like the one who came before him. People persecute him in so many ways. They bother him, they trouble him, they don't let him do his work, which is actually to their benefit. But after he is gone, they will worship him and make him the standard.

Now I blow bubbles with kids. Now people who are around me will make this the standard. The next enlightened being who comes around, if he refuses to blow bubbles, they will say, 'This is not an enlightened being because my master used to blow bubbles with kids. This man doesn't blow bubbles.' (*Laughs*)

This is happening because every conclusion you make – about anything, for that matter – is always coming from the past accumulation in your mind. Whatever kind of accumulation you have, that's the way you go on judging. So based on your different traditions and different backgrounds, accordingly your judgments are made. They don't mean anything.

People around me also naturally get judged because in this culture if you are around a guru you must be like a 'munishwari', you know. (*Laughs*) You must be half-clad, always speak gently, eat only dried apples, not fresh apples (fresh apple is a sin!), and many other things like this. So naturally, people think if somebody is dressing this way, speaking this way, eating this way, doing things the way they are, there can be nothing spiritual about them. But you looking like a munishwari is not important to me. You becoming an ishwar – divine – is important to me.

Everybody can think what they want to think. But when it is necessary to sit down quietly and be with me, let them just do that. Then, in spite of their analysis, in spite of disagreeing with everything that I am as a person, they helplessly want to be here. That's a good way to be here. Now, if all my actions agree with their idea of how a guru should be, then obviously I'm a no-good guru for them. If the guru is trying to fit into the disciples' expectations, he is unfit to be a guru. He will never fit into the disciples' expectations. Disciples will be constantly frustrated with the guru's ways because he won't fit into their expectations.

About whether a guru chooses a disciple or a disciple chooses a guru. A disciple longs to be with the guru. It's the guru who chooses how much and how. And why he chooses the way he chooses, there are so many complex reasons. And for different gurus, it may be different.

That reminds me of Ashtavakra. Ashtavakra literally means,

for those of you who do not know, a man with eight terrible
deformities in his body. Ashtavakra had a deformed body,
but was an enlightened being. Janaka, the king, was also an
enlightened being. He was Ashtavakra's disciple, and when
he got enlightened, he was willing to renounce everything
that he had. But Ashtavakra insisted that Janaka should
remain a king because he felt the people deserve an
enlightened king.

Janaka said, 'All I want is to be with you. I don't want to be
a king.'

But Ashtavakra insisted, 'You be a king. I will spend as much
time with you as possible, but you continue to be the king.
People deserve an enlightened king.'

In Ashtavakra's ashram, there were many sanyasis, training
under him, who always felt a little bothered by the kind of
relationship Janaka held with their guru. If Janaka comes,
Ashtavakra spends hours, sometimes days, with him, just
talking with him, walking with him, just being with him.
One was a master; another, a disciple; both enlightened. But
the sanyasis there were getting bothered by this. They
thought, 'We have given up everything and come. But the
master never bothers to spend that much time with us. King
Janaka is a king; he has a kingdom. He has many wives; he
has all the pleasures of a king, the power of a king,
everything. Once in a way he comes and whenever he comes
he gets total attention from Ashtavakra.' They thought this

just amounts to prejudice, a bias. It was bothering them. Ashtavakra was aware of this.

One day there was a satsangh happening. A whole lot of sanyasis were sitting with the master. Janaka was also sitting in this group. Ashtavakra set up a certain situation. One of the servants – or the help that was in the ashram – came running into the hall where the satsangh was happening and announced that a troop of monkeys had come down and were playing havoc with the sanyasis' clothes, which were drying on the clothesline. All the sanyasis or monks just got up and ran to save their clothes. They retrieved their clothes from the monkeys and came back. And the satsangh continued.

After some time, one of Janaka's guards came rushing into the hall and announced that Janaka's palace was on fire. Janaka immediately admonished the guard. He said, 'How dare you run into this hall when my master is speaking? Get out of here!'

Then Ashtavakra told the monks, 'Your clothes, the kind of clothes you wear, most people in the world wouldn't even touch them. They wouldn't use them as a mop cloth. But when the monkeys were playing with your clothes, you did not even bother to ask me; you just got up and ran. Look at him. His palace is burning, but he only admonishes the guard for entering without permission and disturbing the satsangh. That's the difference. And that's why he gets what he gets, and you get what you get.'

So these people who are always busy making judgments about everything in the world, if they were really peaceful beings we could attach some value to their opinions. They themselves are an absolute mess; so their opinions don't mean anything. They pass opinions, not because of any wisdom; they are quite helpless about it. Whatever they see, they have to say something about it, because all they have is their opinions. What else do they have? Without their opinions, they will be nothing. With their opinions they are a whole mess of nonsense. So it's okay. It's all right for them because they are doing it helplessly. We would like to help them out of it.

You having opinions means you are making sure that you don't experience things the way they are. The moment you hold an opinion, for example, right now about me, you cannot experience me the way I am. Your opinion will block you. That is true with everything in life. The more opinions you have about life, the less you will ever experience life. You are destroying the possibility of being alive. You are destroying the possibility of knowing life. And once you destroy the possibility of knowing life, you certainly destroy the possibility of going beyond; there's no question about that.

So the whole process of what you call 'life' happens as energy. Only your personality is created with your thoughts, ideas, emotions and opinions. Your personality is an unconscious creation of yours. It is your creation but you are so deeply enslaved to it. Do not go on strengthening this unconscious monster that you have created. I call your personality a monster. You may have a very pleasant personality. Especially if your personality is very pleasant and pleasing and you are deeply attached to it, it's a real monster because it kills all possibility of you ever knowing anything beyond the limitations of your person. At least if it's an unpleasant personality, you wouldn't like to be attached to it; you would like and seek to be something else. But if you have evolved a pleasant personality which is well-accepted in the social situations, it takes a whole lifetime or more for a person to realize the falsehood of what he is doing.

So about being judged – once you are born in this world, everybody has a right to judge you. (*Laughs*) It's okay. You cannot stop them from judging. It is just that if you are a spiritual seeker, you don't get into this mess of judging everybody around you because with this you are destroying your possibilities. But somebody else judging you, it's okay. Let them pass their opinions.

'If you want the real thing, stop the 'take-away' business. Simply be.'

Seeker: Sadhguru, I've heard you say, 'Be with me,' quite a few times on this journey. But is it possible for any one to be with you without proper sadhana, without really exhausting his old karmas? And if yes, then how?

Sadhguru: 'Being with me'. First of all, what does it mean? Is it about thinking about someone? Is it about generating thoughts and emotions about them? No. Being with me is about using me as a tool just to be, that's all. Being with me does not mean you have continuous thought or continuous emotion. The psychological processes, all the play of thought and emotions that happens within you, whatever it may be, can only be a means of paving the way. It is not the journey.

Now, you want to go to Coimbatore; if you generate thoughts about going to Coimbatore, it will pave the way. Maybe you will buy a ticket; maybe you will start walking; maybe you will start doing something in that direction; but thinking about it by itself is not going, isn't it? It doesn't matter how much you think about it, you don't go. But by thinking about it, you pave the way. Only because a thought – 'I want to go to Coimbatore' – has come, depending upon how strong that thought is, that quickly you pave your way. But the thought can never be the journey; it is only paving the way.

So when I say, 'Be with me,' initially it may be all about the thought that you generate. Naturally, because that's the way your mind operates. Maybe if the thought becomes strong, it gets followed by emotion. If thought and emotion align with each other, what you are thinking and what you are emoting at a certain time are together, then it becomes a strong rope, a strong connection with something, or a strong possibility that you will go there.

If you are thinking and feeling strongly about something, you will naturally go there. Isn't it so? Whatever that is. Now today you want to go to the Ganges, not the valleys. If you are thinking and also feeling strongly about it, if you start thinking, 'Ganges, Ganges, Ganges' (*Laughter*), and if your heart starts beating, 'Ganges, Ganges, Ganges', invariably you will end up there, isn't it? That thought itself doesn't take you there, but it gives the necessary impetus in you to move in that direction. Still you have to walk to the Ganges. However much you think about it you will not end up in Ganges, isn't it? So thought and emotion are just instruments to pave the way, but never the journey. This is a simple distinction but unfortunately most people do not get this distinction. They think that thinking about something is already being there.

Somebody told you what 'Bhaja Govindam' means? No? 'Go' means cow, and Govinda is one who herds the cows, a cowherd. 'Think of the cowherd' means 'the one who herds the existence'. Now it is not being said that you only need to think about the cowherd. It says 'Moodhamate': "Foolish mind, think about the cowherd". Because only if the mind thinks about the cowherd, will it pave the way for you to walk in that direction. So people asked you to think about

God not because it is a reality, but because by thinking about it, it will set a direction to your life, that's all. So when I say, 'Be with me', I am not telling you sit there and think about me. That's a pretty bad thought. (*Laughter*)

Once you have made an attempt to be in a certain space, a certain possibility has become a live factor. It is no more a thought. There is a certain live possibility. A certain investment of energy has been made. Unfortunately, psychological exercises on the planet are just passing off as spiritual processes, where there is no investment of life, where there is no activation of life. It is all about thought and emotion. It will just go on as a psychological process. Psychological process means it is your creation. Yes? Isn't it your creation? If you get too involved in your own creation, you will miss the Creator's creation, obviously. That's what is happening right now. Whether you are thinking about Sadhguru or God or the Devil, it doesn't matter; if you get into too much of psychological process, it is your creation. If you get too enamored with your own creation, you will miss the Creator's creation.

This is the only source of misery if you really look at it. This is the only source of confusion in people. Confusion is only in your mind, isn't it? There is no confusion in the creation. Confusion is only in the mind because you have attached too much importance to the psychological process. It is your creation. When your creation has gained so much significance, naturally you get completely dislocated from the Creator's creation. That means that from reality, you are moving into the hallucinatory. Whether the hallucination is about God or guru or cinema or money or whatever, it doesn't matter. Whether it is a good hallucination or a bad hallucination, whether you are having a wonderful dream or a nightmare, they are the same, isn't it? You are getting entangled with the unreal.

So being with me is not thinking about me, not emoting about me, but simply being. Once you made this mistake of sitting in situations like this (you can leave even now!) (*Laughs*), if you allow yourself to be, you can only be with me. There is no other way. Whether you think about me or you think about something, it really is not of great consequence. Maybe in terms of paving the way; yes. What you think about and what you feel about is where you naturally go. In that context, yes. But existentially, it doesn't mean anything. You thinking about something doesn't mean anything, because it has no existential substance to it. It is purely psychological.

So how to be with me? The only way you know how to be is to see, to hear, to be focused. Now for many of you over a period of time, if I say, 'Be with me,' the first thing you do is close your eyes. This you don't do consciously: 'Okay, now closing my eyes is superior to opening my eyes.' It will not work that way. It is just that what you held as external has become internal. Naturally, you close your eyes. If it happens naturally, it's fine. If you pretend, it is a waste of life.

The problem with spiritual processes is just this: somebody did that, so everybody wants to do that. By imitating that act, the spiritual process will not happen. Now, Gautama sat like this, absolutely still. You try to sit like this – it won't work. Chaitanya Mahaprabhu danced, so you dance like him – it won't help. Somebody else worked all his life through, so you do that – it won't help. There are many other mystics who did many freaky things. If you do it, it won't help.

On a certain day, Adi Shankara was walking as usual and his disciples were walking behind him. They were passing through a village and there was a shop which was selling arrack, the locally brewed liquor. Adi Shankara just walked in, took a pot full of arrack, just drank it up and walked on. Then the disciples were walking behind him and the discussions started among them: 'Our guru is drinking; why are we missing out?' If he is drinking, that means it is the right thing, yes?

The next village came and all these guys ran into the arrack shop and drank, and they were wobbling behind him. So Adi Shankara saw in the rearview mirror (*Laughter*) that his disciples had rubbery legs and were walking in a wobbly way. When the next village came, he went to the blacksmith's shop. There the blacksmith had molten iron. Shankara just picked it up, drank it, and walked on. Now they all straightened up. (*Laughter*) This they don't want to do. (*Laughs*)

So just imitating an act is the main reason why you are unable to be. Right from your childhood they have told you to emulate somebody else. This is the main reason why people can't be, you know. Especially the press people, when they come, they ask, 'Who is your role model?' I say, 'What is that? I never heard of anything like that. What is a role model?' 'No, no,' they insist. 'Who is your role model?' That means whom do you imitate? (*Laughs*) Or who inspired you? Maybe that's what they are asking. It's most important that your children grow up without a role model. And it's especially important that it's not you. (*Laughter*)

We always think we must set up a role model. If you set up a role model, that's a desperate effort to be something other than what you are. In this effort, this natural quality of being is completely lost in a human being. He is always desperately trying to be something other than what he is, which takes away his ability to simply be. Generally, this is a common question that keeps coming to me, particularly from the older generation of people, who have desperately been trying to be spiritual. They've been to all the Gita discourses; they've heard Vedanta; they've heard many things. They believe they know all these things better than Krishna himself. But they come here and they look around and see. After some time, they realize these young people who don't know a damn thing about any spirituality are jumping and flying away, but they are just sitting and watching.

This question comes to me any number of times. 'I have done so much. I have always wanted this in my life. Nothing is happening to me. I can see these young boys and girls. They don't know a damn thing, but they are flying away. What is it?' (*Laughs*) This is all the problem is; you are desperately trying to be something other than who you are, which just destroys the very way you are. Role models you have; too much imitation has gone into you. Imitation involves tremendous calculation, isn't it? If you want to imitate somebody, you can never imitate anybody totally. You want to improve upon your imitation too, isn't it? So imitation involves tremendous calculation. Once this calculation comes, you cannot be.

One simple way of learning to be is you just drop this one calculation, 'What can I get out of this satsangh?' You just drop that. You don't have to get anything, okay? You don't have to benefit from this. Just waste half a day and go. (*Laughter*) Really. 'What should I get out of my meditation?' Nothing. Just waste fifteen-twenty minutes every day. So do not meditate; just learn to waste some time. Nothing needs to happen. This is not about resting; this is not about becoming healthy; this is not about becoming enlightened; this is not about reaching heaven. All this is just wasting time. When you are not trying to be anything, not trying to get anywhere, you are being.

This is all modern terminology: 'What is the 'take-away' from today's satsangh?' (*Laughter*) If you look for 'take-away', you will only take petty things; the real thing will never come with you. If you want the real thing, stop the 'take-away' business. Simply be. Nothing needs to happen.

See, because people do not have the necessary awareness to simply be, an alternative was suggested, which is you just be in love. This is because this is one state where, to some extent, you can be without a take-away. But that's not true, generally. Even though you think you are in love with somebody, if they don't give what they are supposed to give, it will all crack up. Isn't it so? Generally, a love affair is just a mutual benefit scheme, isn't it? (*Laughter*) 'You give me this, I will give you that. If you don't give me that, I won't give you this.' Yes or no?

All these talks about developing a deep sense of love or compassion are only towards the end of taking away the expectation. 'What should I get?' is being removed by creating a strong sense of emotion towards somebody. Otherwise, the mind is calculating, 'That's okay, why should I do this? What will I get?' It's just to remove that, that's all. Otherwise, by itself it doesn't mean anything. So, no take-away today. Is it okay? You won't get anything. 'So is this the last satsangh I will come to?' (*Laughter*) Yes. Because, 'If I don't get anything, what the hell am I doing here?' That's the nature of your mind, please see.

It is so simple. If you drop this one calculation – 'what will

I get?' – ninety per cent of the work is over. Do you understand? Another ten per cent will happen by itself. You know the 'snakes and ladders' game? Many ladders, many snakes, many up-and-down journeys will happen. But once you hit the last rung, no more snakes. You just have to take one step and then another and another, and you are there, isn't it? But no more snakes to eat you up. This is just like that. If you just drop this one calculation of 'what can I get', after that, no more snakes!

It is just a question of time. You will get there. If from everything in your life, 'what can I get', is dropped, it means you will become really boundless and absolutely compassionate in your life. There is no other way. You just have to drop this one simple calculation, because that is the key to your whole mind and your mental process. That is the key to all the activity that's happening in the mind. You just pull the plug, and it's over. Then being is just natural. How else to be? You are only being even now; you are missing it because of too much psychological activity, isn't it? You can't try to be; it doesn't work. You just have to pull this one plug, 'What can I get?' At least lower it, if you can't pull it out totally. Just lower that and you will see, you will be.

Seeker: Sadhguru, I was once told, 'Do your practices consistently because the way your guru can reach out to you is through your practices.' What does that really mean?

Sadhguru: Now, whether it was said by somebody, or you just overheard it, or you just imagined it – whichever way, it's relevant, so let's talk about it. What has doing your practice got to do with guru reaching out? This simple practice that you have learned – one thing that you have clearly seen is that definitely it makes you much more sensitive and available. If your energies are not open and available, there is not much room for anybody reaching out to you, not just the guru. Even life cannot reach out to you, because you miss everything when your energies are stuck and in certain patterns, which have happened because of certain ways of living and certain karmic structures, and so many things. So, if anybody has to reach out to you, it's important that you have an open enough system. And for your physiology and your psychology to be open, it's very important that your energy system is in a certain level of preparedness and openness.

So doing the practices definitely makes you so much more receptive. Otherwise it's like your cell phone is right now not charged, but I want to call you. What to do? I will go on dialing, but you won't receive it. So it's better to keep your cell phone charged! Similarly, it's better to keep your system charged and open, so that it can easily receive.

And it is also one simple way of you expressing your dedication to the path that you have taken. If that is not there, then there is no focus and there is no receptivity again. I want you to understand, the nature of life is such that only what you are truly focused on (energy-wise especially; mind-wise, body-wise, also it is true, but especially energy-wise), whichever direction you are oriented towards, only that will happen to you. So the practices are a simple way of orienting your energy to a higher possibility.

If your energies are truly open, your guru — even Shiva — has to reach out; he cannot help it. If your energies have really become an invitation to the divine, even the divine cannot refuse you; it's impossible. Even if the guru does not want to reach out, he cannot help it if your energies are so inviting. So all that you are doing with your practices, on one dimension — there are other dimensions of health, well-being, all that — is that you are becoming an invitation to the Divine. So yes, it's very true; keeping your practices going has a lot to do with how much you are available.

'When you sit in a satsangh,…don't worry about what's happening to somebody; be absolutely with me.'

Seeker: During the past few days, in certain processes conducted at the satsanghs, you asked us to focus between the eyebrows. Certain experiences seemed to happen to some people. I don't know what happened and why. I don't know what my problem is. I don't understand why I am unable to experience anything. Please explain.

Sadhguru: You should keep the focus between *your* eyebrows. (*Laughter*)

Seeker: Yes, I understand that. Still I could not experience anything.

Sadhguru: (*Laughs*) I thought you kept it on somebody else's eyebrows. (*Laughter*) Now, satsangh means a communion with truth. You don't know what truth is; so how to commune with it, isn't it? People have been talking about it; the scriptures have been screaming about it; but you do not know what truth is. So right now, when you sit with a guru, he is the nearest thing to truth that you know. That also you are not sure of. See, as far as you are concerned, you are not sure whether he is in truth or not. All you can see is he seems to be at least on a little higher level of existence than you are. That's a reality; let's admit it. You don't know whether he is in truth or not. He may be, he may not be; but you have no way of knowing, isn't it? The only thing that you can recognize is he seems to be much clearer than you about everything. He seems to be more in control of everything than you are. He seems to be at least one step higher than wherever you think you are. So that's why you look up to him.

Right now, let's say we are expecting a flood. You are sitting here in the depression, and you cannot see what's coming. Somebody sitting on that pole up there, every five minutes you would ask him, 'Where is it? What is happening?' Isn't it? He may not be seeing the whole world, but he is sitting in a more elevated place than you are. He may be on top of the world; that you do not know. You have no way of knowing. So let's go with reality. Let's not go with hallucinations; let's not go with belief systems. Let's not simply believe something because those beliefs will crash somewhere. Only reality will sustain itself.

That's the reason why you are sitting with a guru. You don't know whether you will get to the end of the world or beyond the world. But at least you want to get there where he is, to the next peak. So when you sit in a satsangh, sit totally with me. Don't worry about what's happening to somebody; be absolutely with me. Somebody screams, somebody yells, somebody does whatever nonsense they want; that's not your business. Your business is just to be with me. But you are too concerned about what's happening around you. Nothing will ever happen to you, because you have no focus.

See, there are different kinds of material in the world. Now, if I strike a match and keep it here, maybe John's shawl will catch fire so much more easily than his T-shirt, yes? Definitely more easily than the marble on which you are sitting; definitely much more easily than the steel pole that is standing there. Isn't it so? So the question is not whether the shawl is better than the marble, or the steel; that's not the point. This catches fire so much more easily; that's all it is. So you don't worry who is catching fire, who is not catching fire; your business is just to be totally there, for the purpose you are there.

You've heard of Dronacharya, that man who took away somebody's thumb? He is supposed to be the ultimate guru in archery, or any kind of arms, for that matter. These 105 brothers are his disciples. You know, the hundred Kauravas and the five Pandavas. Out of these 105, Arjuna became his favorite disciple to whom he revealed most. Arjuna became the greatest archer. Why this is so is not because Dronacharya played favorites, but simply because nobody else had the quality to receive.

One day they were in a class. They lived in an ashram along with Dronacharya. He was saying something about archery. For practical laboratory work, he took them outside. (*Laughs*) He had set up a toy parrot on the topmost branch of the tree. He took them out and one by one he told them, 'There's a little spot on the neck of the parrot. Aim at that spot and shoot.' When they drew their bow, they waited till he said shoot. He kept them waiting for a few minutes. Most people cannot keep their focus in one place for more than a few seconds. Have you noticed this with yourself? So he let them wait for a few minutes with their bows drawn. It's a strenuous thing, physically, holding it and being focused. Then he asked them, 'What do you see?' Then they went about describing all the leaves on the tree, the fruits, the flowers, the bird, and even the sky. When Arjuna's turn came, he focused and he drew his bow.

Dronacharya asked, 'What do you see?'

Arjuna said, 'Just one spot on the neck of the parrot. That's all I see.'

This man gets somewhere. People without focus, if they get anywhere, it's only accidentally, isn't it? Not because of themselves; in spite of themselves, people get somewhere because so many forces in the existence take them on. But this man will get somewhere because of himself.

So when you are in a satsangh, that's how you must be. You don't worry about what's happening with the rest of the world. You simply be where you have to be, focused on what you have to be. Then what has to happen will happen. What happens to somebody need not happen to you; but what has to happen to you will definitely happen; nobody can deny it to you. But you are so concerned about what's happening to somebody else that time goes waste; life goes waste.

'A little sense of insufficiency; that is why you have come. When you feel absolutely, utterly insufficient, that's when you will know.'

Seeker: But why is it that the very sight of you makes some people go through different states, like yelling and screaming?

Sadhguru: You are not one of them! (*Laughs*)

Seeker: Why does it happen? And does it mean that they do not have control over their minds?

Sadhguru: Oh, you've already made the conclusion that they don't have any control over their minds. Now, if you have not noticed this, they don't even have to see me. If I just come walking there, even if they are sitting with their eyes closed, they will go crazy. Have you noticed this?

Seeker: Yes.

Sadhguru: So it's not a visual effect. (*Laughs*) It is just like, when the sun comes up in the morning, many flowers bloom. But those buds which are unable to bloom – no wonder those haven't bloomed. Those flowers which bloomed, they wither after some time, you know? So when they bloom and wither, those which could not bloom will think that they have lost control over their life. They have bloomed and they withered (*Laughs*), but they wither to become something else. A flower becomes a fruit or a seed, and life moves into the next dimension of experience and existence.

So never make judgments about things which are not in your experience. It will be very foolish, because all your judgments come from your present experience of life, isn't it? So anything that is not in your experience, if it is not okay in your mind, you are ensuring that nothing new ever happens to you. Do you understand what I am saying? From this limited present experience, if you go on making judgments – that these other people are not okay, that they are weak-minded – you will find that you have been worshipping many on this list of weak-minded people. Shall I tell you many names that you have been worshipping? In your list of weak-minded people, the foremost among them are Ramakrishna Paramahamsa, all the gopis around the Krishna (*Laughs*), Shiva himself (a very weak-minded man – he always burst forth into all kinds of ecstatic states!) and all the people around Shiva.

It is just that life happens on many different levels and dimensions. Right now your experience is limited to just a few aspects of life. Before you fall dead, would you like to explore all the possibilities that life has?

Seeker: Yes.

Sadhguru: Then you should not make judgments about things which are not in your experience. It is not that they are weak-minded people. It is just that, when I am around, they are completely mindless people. If you don't have a mind, the question of 'weak mind/ strong mind' doesn't arise. I want you to understand, the mind is a very weak instrument, anyway. It's capable of doing incredible things, but only in one dimension. If you switch your life to another dimension, it is completely useless. In the process of your survival, in the process of looking good in society, it's a great instrument. In the process of approaching the divine, it's no good.

So if your whole life is about just looking good, then the mind is a great instrument; you can worship it. If your life is about knowing the unbounded, if your life is about knowing the very limits of who you are, if your life is about knowing the very source of what you are, then your mind cannot explore these dimensions. So some people keep their mind aside and they become mindless. They don't care what you think about them. They will scream and yell and roll and shake (*Laughs*). Some of them are screaming too much; we have knocked them on their heads and set them right. But don't make judgments about things that you do not know. That's a sure way to ignorance. It simply means you are enshrining your ignorance. So what's happening to them? Would you like to explore and see?

Seeker: Yes.

Sadhguru: See, somebody is shaking; you don't know what's happening — whether they are shivering with cold or medication... (*Laughter*) Only if you experience it, you know. So make yourself available; we'll see. Make yourself receptive. If you want to know something beyond what you are right now, one thing is you must see that the way you are right now is not sufficient. You must understand that unless there is a strong feeling of insufficiency, you will not seek anything big; you will not seek anything with great intensity.

You know, these days people are teaching you all this nonsense, that you must keep telling yourself, 'I am great, I am wonderful.' Yes? This is called self-esteem. You keep telling your children, 'You are great, I love you. Don't worry; everything is fine. You are just on top of the world.' This is just bullshit. It is just a way of enshrining your limitations. Now, first of all, why does somebody have to tell you that you are great, or why do you have to tell yourself that you are great? Because there is a sense of insufficiency, isn't it? If you are feeling insufficient, I think it's very good. Only when you strongly feel a sense of insufficiency, you will long for something bigger to happen in your life. If you try to hide your insufficiency in cruddy words, then you will never long for anything. You will go on telling yourself everything is wonderful the way it is.

It is not that we don't enjoy life the way it is, but it is not enough. Only then you long for more, isn't it? Just eating pongal, drinking coffee and (*simulates a belch*) is not sufficient for you. For many people it's sufficient, isn't it? For many people that's the ultimate in life. It feels good, pongal and coffee together, I know. (*Laughter*) Quite a good combination for lethargy. For many people that's the ultimate satisfaction in their life.

Only when you feel this eating, drinking, sleeping is not enough – that all these little things that I do in my life are not enough; that I want to know something more; all this is not sufficient for me – an intensity of longing for another dimension of life comes. Otherwise, it won't happen. So right now that's all you need to do with yourself, instead of making judgments about other people. Of these screaming people, some of them may be ecstatic and highly meditative, some just insane. It doesn't matter, you know?

We are okay with both people. I have no problems. Whether they are meditative or they are mad, both ways it's okay with me. I know what to do with both people.

Now I want you to understand, when you don't know the ABC of your life – when you don't know where you come from; where you will go; when you don't know the very substance you are made of – you making judgments about life is also madness, isn't it? So don't get into that madness. If you truly want to be receptive to dimensions which are beyond your present level of experience, one thing that you have to do with yourself is to simply see how insufficient you are, as you are right now. Just see, there is no substance to you. You think you are something. You are nothing really. This inhalation, exhalation that's going on – if the next inhalation doesn't happen, you're done, isn't it?

You just look at the mountains as you go. You know, they can swallow you up in no time. (*Laughs*) You may be thinking many things about you, but still you don't know the fundamental substance of what you are, isn't it? If just yoga is another kind of entertainment for you, that's another karma. It's okay. People can go on with it. But if you really want to grow, one simple thing that you can do with yourself is just see how stupid you are. Not knowing the previous step, not knowing the next step, your entanglement in the present step of life is so tremendous, isn't it? You don't know the previous step; you don't know the next step. But this step that you are in, you are stuck in it so badly, as if this is the beginning and end of life.

Now you just have to see, what you consider 'myself' is not even substance. What you consider 'myself' is just a bundle of thoughts, ideas, opinions, belief-systems. So one by one, I want you to see that, 'My thoughts are stupid; my judgments are stupid; my emotions are stupid; my ideas are stupid; my philosophies are stupid; my belief systems are stupid. Everything that I know as 'myself' is utterly stupid, and I am the greatest idiot in the world.' The moment you see this, now every cell in your body will be open to know what is what. If you see everything about you is utterly stupid, then suddenly you find every cell in your body is open to receive. That's all you need to do. That's what we have been doing to you from day one. Since you came to Isha Yoga, you have been feeling like an idiot, isn't it? Very gently, very lovingly, they have been making you feel like an utter idiot. Isn't it so?

Seeker: We already feel a sense of insufficiency and that is why we have come to you.

Sadhguru: A little sense of insufficiency; that is why you have come. When you feel absolutely, utterly insufficient, that's when you will know. A little insufficiency has brought you here; utter insufficiency will deliver you.

Part Four

Walking the Spiritual Path

*'Every moment, whatever you step on, in many
ways, you are only stepping on me.'*

The journey is arduous, the path steep and craggy, and the destination often seems like 'a conspiracy of cartographers'. When does it all end? Is the road as interminable as it seems? And why did one set out on this crazy expedition in the first place? As the questions grow insistent, the guru, in his compassion, responds.

He speaks with an insider's understanding of the seeker's thirst, the yearning, the Himalayan lust that is just 'life's longing for itself'. He speaks with equal empathy of doubt — that recurrent hurdle on the road to self-discovery. He speaks of the many tricks of the mind, its ingenious strategies for self-perpetuation. He speaks of the two options available to all seekers — complete inclusion and complete exclusion. He speaks of flowers, those mystical symbols of spontaneous non-utilitarian beauty. He speaks of how the guru's blessings are not about thought or emotion, but a simple infusion of 'gasoline in the car'. He speaks of how truth is not an idea, but an infection; how a guru is essentially a transmitter, not a teacher.

And he urges the fearful travelers to relinquish strategies of self-preservation, to allow the journey to break them rather than make them. 'The seed goes through the tremendous struggle of losing itself...,' he says. 'But without that vulnerability, without the breaking, without the shedding of the shell, life won't sprout.'

Or yet again: 'You must burst and go crazy with the mountains... You must simply crack open.'

And in the background, the Himalayas wait — mysterious, majestic, eternally patient.

'This thirst to know is not created by you; it is just life longing for itself.'

When you walk the spiritual path, your biggest enemy is the huge sense of doubt that will periodically arise. It's like a menstrual cycle; it keeps coming at regular periods for people. If you watch it, there is a pattern to this; it keeps coming back at certain times. 'Am I just wasting my time? Am I missing out on life, doing all this spiritual nonsense?' These things keep coming back, yes? (*Laughs*)

So the very basic purpose of being in the Himalayan spaces is this: being with people who are on the path and also making yourself available to situations and spaces which you cannot create by yourself. Periodically, most people – except people who are firmly on the path – need some kind of confirmation, some kind of guarantee that, yes, there is something. So the Himalayan trek is an attempt in that direction – to confirm that there is something beyond what you know. Something much more than what you know.

So once you strongly feel that, wanting to know is very human and natural. You don't have to really create the want. If you realise that you do not know, the wanting to know naturally arises within you. This thirst to know is not created by you; it is just life longing for itself. Life will not settle unless it knows itself.

So you just have to become aware of your ignorance. The

thirst for enlightenment will anyway come into life. You cannot kill it. Many of you have been trying to kill it in so many ways. You have not been able to kill it, isn't it? (*Laughs*) You have been trying to spoil the soup in many ways for yourself, haven't you? But still it does not stop because this has not been inspired by somebody. The moment you become aware of your ignorance, the quest for knowing is just natural. It need not be taught to you; it need not be inspired in you. The only thing the guru has to make you realize is that you really don't know. In his presence, when you feel utterly dumb and stupid, then the longing to know will get fired up.

(*Laughs*) So that reminds me. It so happened that two Christian missionaries went deep into Africa. They were captured by a cannibal tribe that prepared a huge cauldron, made these two missionaries stand in the vessel and set fire to the vessel to cook them alive and eat them. One of them was shivering and crying, 'Jesus, my Lord, come and save me!'

The other one was looking around at everybody. The cannibals were just dancing in great joy that they had found food. The missionary started laughing. The weeping missionary looked at him and said, 'What are you laughing about, John? You're going to be cooked alive. What are you laughing about? It looks like our Lord has failed us.'

So John, the missionary, said, 'The best thing is these

bloody savages don't know that I just pissed in their soup."
(*Laughter*)

So please don't piss in your own soup, okay? You are capable
of doing it. That is why I am reminding you.

So if some kind of confirmation has happened to you in
some way, you just have to intensify that and keep steadily
on the focus. You may say, 'Oh, I have been with Isha for
five years.' That's not the point. In twenty-four hours, how
many moments are your mind, body, energy and emotion
focused towards your spiritual well-being? How many
moments? That's what you need to look at. You must make
an account of it and see how to improve it on a daily basis.
In twenty-four hours, how many moments are my body, my
mind, my emotion and energy moving in the same direction?
If these four are moving in four different directions,
obviously you are not going to go anywhere.

Your mind is in spirituality, your emotion is strongly with
your family, or something else. Your body wants to go to
the restaurant, your energy — you know where. When you
are like this, spirituality will just remain a dream and an
entertainment. Only when all these four dimensions are
focused in one direction, movement happens. Transformation happens. You start moving. If you look at yourself,
even during those fifteen or thirty minutes of practice, only
for a few moments are all these four things are focused in
one direction, isn't it? Those are the fruitful moments. The

rest of the moments are just imagination. If you just increase
the quantum of those moments in your day-to-day life, then
you will see an enormous transformation within you.

We don't count in years; we count in moments. We want
to know in a day's time for how many moments all of you
is focused in one direction. So one 'take-away' from the
Himalayas has to be that. You just have to keep a count of
your spiritual moments in a day. If you increase those, it's
pretty easy to get there. Only twenty-four hours in a day.
Not a big number, is it?

Somebody — I forget his name — who was very dear to
Ramakrishna Paramahamsa, went to him and said, 'Oh,
Bhagawan, I just want to be with you all the time. But I
have a wife; I have children; I have to earn money; I have to
go to my office. I really don't know what to do. My heart
is here, but I am putting my body elsewhere. My suffering
is unbearable. What should I do?' Ramakrishna had his own
way of expressing himself. He said, 'Just the utterance of
the name 'Kali', if it brings tears to your eyes, you forget
about your earning, your job, your other responsibilities. You
just forget about all of it. Do not worry. She will take care
of it.'

Similarly, if just the mention of your guru's name brings
tears to your eyes, I would say the same. But I don't say
those things to you because I am very embarrassed about
who I am. If I go into detail, it would be too fairytale-ish

and incredible for you.

Every moment, whatever you step on, in many ways, you are only stepping on me. It is just that when a little awareness of that enters you, you should burst. You should become ripe, and be ready to sprout. A seed is a certain comfort because it has integrity; it has a shell; it has protection. But if a seed is not broken, a new sprout will never happen. If you try to save the shield that protects the seed, no new life will ever happen; no new possibility will ever come. You just put the seed in the earth and you forget about it. After a few days you just see a plant and you are happy. But the seed goes through the tremendous struggle of losing itself – losing its safety and integrity and becoming vulnerable to every outside force that's around. But without that vulnerability, without the breaking, without the shedding of the shell, life won't sprout.

It is not that it is different now where you are standing. It is not different in Chennai either. It is just that a little awareness brings a completely new possibility into your life. It is when you travel with various kinds of people with many limitations, you understand who you really are. You may deceive yourself; you may believe you are many things which you are not, when you are living in the comfort of your home. But it is different when you have to face situations which are different, when you have to face people who are very different from what you think a human being should be, and they happen to sit with you for twenty days. Everything about

them is different – the way they eat; the way they blow their
nose; the way they go to the toilet. When somebody who is
an alien in your perception, sits next to you, to travel with
him gently, lovingly, joyfully, is your growth. You know, that
means that you are growing beyond your limitations.

'In stagnation, there is no safety.'

Seeker: But, Sadhguru, it's not easy to grow beyond our
limitations. Interactions can be trying, relationships can be
challenging. How can we love people who irritate us?

Sadhguru: How to love people who irritate you? Don't
pretend to love them; just understand that they're irritating
you. Why are they irritating you? Simply because they are
not the way you expect them to be; they're not the way you
want them to be. But in the same breath you also claim that
you believe in God. If you believe in God, the person who
irritates you also happens to be a creation of God, and he
seems to be such a masterpiece that he can just irritate the
hell out of you, isn't it? So don't deceive yourself. Just see,
the irritation is happening because you have already decided
what is right and what is wrong. You have decided that the
way you see it is the right way to be.

If people are different from you, they will first irritate you.
Then you will get angry; then you will hate them; then you
will want to kill them. These are all natural processes. It
happens simply because you are expecting everybody in the

world to be like you. If everybody in the world were like you, could you be here? In your own home, if there was one more person like you, could you live in that house? Would it be possible?

It's very good that everybody in the world is the way they are. Any human being that you take here out of this whole mass of people is absolutely unique, isn't it? The person who is sitting next to you right now, if you look at him, you will see that there is no other human being like him anywhere on this planet. There never was one and there never will be one such person. This is an absolutely unique human being. If you recognize that there is only one like this, that he is such precious material, how can he irritate you? And it is such a miracle for you that today you are sitting next to this unique human being. If you see this, where is the question of irritation?

You're blind; that is why you are irritated. You're simply blind to life. You have not opened your eyes and looked at life. Otherwise, how can anybody irritate you?

Questioner: Sadhguru, you've talked of how a seed has to go through the pain of losing its safety. You've said that it has to become vulnerable in order to sprout. Until the sprouting happens, do seekers have to live their lives in increased states of fragility and vulnerability? Isn't that particularly hard on them?

Sadhguru: Oh, the seed, in making itself vulnerable, is not forsaking its safety. Its only safety is in its sprouting, growing and multiplying. That's the only safety. If you do not know this, the more insecure a particular population on the planet feels, the more they will reproduce. You know this? The poorer societies on the planet always have a higher rate of reproduction than the more affluent classes on the planet, because there is a certain insecurity about their existence. So the safety lies not in remaining a seed; the safety lies in sprouting, growing and multiplying. So you are not forsaking your safety by becoming vulnerable or by becoming available to change.

Once a man came and told his friend, 'A long time ago, I was an invalid.' His friend asked, 'What's your problem? You mean you were an invalid?' 'No till I was one year of age, I was an invalid: I was crawling.' (*Laughs*) Your childhood, or even before that, is like being a seed. If you did not sprout and grow would you be safer? You would be an invalid. I know these days it's become fashionable for people to claim, 'I am like a child.' Even the so-called spiritual people are going about claiming, 'I am a child.' If you say, 'I am a child', don't think it is some celebrated status. When you say, 'I am a child', you are saying, 'I did not grow up'. Let us say your mind remained stagnant from the age of three, but only your body has grown. So what are we to call you? Spiritual? Or...I don't want to use harsh words, but naturally people would say, 'He is mentally retarded (*Laughs*), handicapped – or an invalid.'

So there is no safety in stagnation. A seed is meaningful only for a certain span of time, but to remain a seed is stagnation. Seed is life, potential life, and that's very important. But if you try to keep anything in a state of stagnation, for sure you will lose it. The only safety is to make it grow. The only safety is to make it sprout and prosper. Whether it's your body or your mind or your life, the only safety is in allowing it to grow, not in trying to preserve it. Try this with your body and see. Many of you have tried, haven't you? Because you want to live for a long time, from tomorrow onwards, eat all the best food and save the body; don't use it. If you want we can provide you a coffin, because anyway you will need it very soon. There is no safety in trying to save the body; that's not the way life is made. The only way to save it is to use it. So the only way a seed can be safe is for it to sprout and become a plant and a tree; that is the only way there is safety for the seed. In stagnation, there is no safety.

But your mind would speak otherwise. Your mind would always say a seed is safe because generally it's in a hard case and it looks more solid, more preservable. A plant out there is vulnerable. Anybody can stamp on it; any animal can grab it and eat it up. But that's not how life happens.

A young boy came home one day and told his father, 'Daddy, I have some good news for you.'

His father asked, 'What is the good news?'

The boy said, 'You know I took the math test.'

The father said, 'Yes, what happened?'

'You said if I pass the math test, you are going to give me two thousand rupees. The good news is you saved two thousand rupees.' (*Laughter*)

That's not safety! (*Laughter*)

'Isha is not an establishment; Isha is not an organization. Isha is... just a tool for one's growth.'

Seeker: It looks like I can't turn myself in right away. I still have parts of myself that have to wear away and wither out. How can I offer myself to Isha in the meantime?

Sadhguru: Now, did you all understand the question? The question is, 'Sadhguru, you know I still have investments in the world – in money, in emotion and so many things. (*Laughs*) I still have things to wear out, so how can I offer myself to Isha?'

First, you need to understand that Isha is not an establishment; Isha is not an organization. Isha is a tool; it is just a tool for one's growth. This must be very clear. It is not an organization or a religion or a cult. It is just a tool, a device, which has been carefully crafted so that it works for every kind of person who comes there. It's a threshing mill. Otherwise how to get the grain out?

So how to offer yourself to Isha? Totally. There is no other way. Does it mean that I must come and live at the Velliangiri foothills? Not necessarily. That is a choice. But if you want to offer yourself, the husk in you has to be beaten out. You can't stand away from the threshing-mill and get the grain out, isn't it? If the grain has to come out and the husk has to be shed, you have to go through the threshing mill. Do I have to be physically in a particular place? No. Isha is not physically limited to any particular place. But your offering has to be total. Half of you getting in doesn't work.

If you just put one hand into the threshing mill, it's going to be a very painful process, an extremely painful process, and of course you will come to the wrong conclusion that anyway nothing comes out of it. Nothing will come out of it, if you give half, or a quarter, or three-fourths of yourself. Only if you give yourself totally, something will come out of it.

Giving yourself totally need not necessarily mean you have to be in a particular place and do a particular thing. Wherever you are, you can give yourself totally. It is just that you are educating yourself because this is also about you realizing your Isha-ness. Isha means the divine, the boundless divine. So, you are running a family right now; that is also toward realizing yourself. You are doing a business right now; that is also toward realizing yourself. If everything in your life is hundred per cent dedicated towards your realization and nothing is spared – your family, your profession, your life, your everything – then you have offered yourself to Isha.

Now if you have your spirituality and the rest of your life separate, then you don't know what life is. Then you are like a person who puts one hand into the threshing-mill and hopes something will come out. All that will come out is suffering. Suffering matures people, or maybe takes you unawares. If you keep one hand in unawareness, one day you will get sucked in. The possibilities are there, but it's a stupid way of doing things. If everything becomes towards one purpose, only then something wonderful will come out of it.

'You can truly involve yourself with life only when you are not identified with it.'

Seeker: If I don't identify myself with my thoughts and with a situation, will I be able to give myself fully to the situation and do the needful?

Sadhguru: See, logically, not identifying yourself with something looks like there is a distance between you and what you are doing. But non-identification need not necessarily mean non-involvement. In fact, when you are not identified, you can consciously involve yourself. The only reason that you cannot involve yourself totally – that you cannot throw yourself into every situation that happens in your life – is that you are so deeply identified. You have become like a vested interest, so you cannot give yourself totally. But when you are not identified with it, you can by choice involve yourself absolutely, because you're not identified with it.

Right now, in a situation like this – a few people just sitting in a relaxed atmosphere – if you choose, you can just involve yourself without any inhibition. That's because you're not identified. There's nothing to be lost, nothing to be gained. You can just throw yourself into it. But when you are identified, each time your involvement questions and threatens who you are and what you are. So every situation – if it is not going the way you think it should be going – your very identity is threatened; it becomes a very insecure and fearful situation for you. Once you go through this experience, your whole sense of involvement will come down. You become subdued, less involved with life. You can truly involve yourself with life only when you are not identified with it. That goes both for thought and the situations in which we live.

Seeker: So if I don't identify myself with the situation, are you saying that I will be able to do what is needed? I am wondering if I will then be able to involve myself completely in that particular situation. Suppose something happens to one of my family members, maybe I'll do what I can to help him or her. But if I am not attached to the situation, you think I will involve myself day and night helping the person?

Sadhguru: Now, if something did happen to one of your loved ones, if you are not identified with it, you will do everything to the best of your ability. Your affection is not gone just because you are not identified. But if you are identified with it, you won't sleep; you won't eat; you won't do the things that you could have done properly. So you tell me, which is the best way to be? To retain all your faculties and capabilities, or to lose them? Which is right?

It is just that ignorant people have always made you believe that if somebody near and dear to you is sick, or dead, you must be broken and incapacitated; otherwise you don't love them. It's not true. Love does not mean incapacitation. Love is a capability. Love is an involvement. Love is a commitment. It's not necessary that you should be broken. If you dissolve, it's fine. If you are broken, you are broken simply because you are identified, not because you are involved.

You feel guilty for not being broken; that's the problem, isn't it? (*Laughs*) You feel guilty for enjoying life. You feel guilty for being alive. You feel guilty for being joyful. Somebody is sick back at home, and you are laughing – you must feel guilty about it. It's just nonsense. One person is sick, so the whole world need not be sick. If one person is sick, it's very important that the rest of the house is joyful, isn't it? Which is better for your family? One person in the family is sick right now. Is it better that all of you are joyful and do the best that you can do for that person, or that all of you also become sick in empathy?

Seeker: The sick person can be hurt that everyone around is joyous, while he or she is having such a hard time. Wouldn't that hurt much more?

Sadhguru: So now, what you're talking about is mentally sick people. (*Laughs*) If somebody is ill in some way, he needs injections of joy, not injections of misery. Now, you are not joyous at his cost; you are joyous for him. If somebody is ill, you must create an atmosphere of joy and well-being. But always cultures have made this mistake: if somebody is ill, you create an atmosphere of ill health and misery around him. If you are really concerned about people around you, the best thing you can do is always to create an atmosphere of health and well-being, not of misery and ill health. So if he is worried that somebody else is joyous, his problem is not his illness; he's got some other problem which needs to be addressed.

'If you go on aspiring to somehow kill the mind or to avoid the mind, it will be a futile effort.'

Seeker: Sadhguru, do I have the choice, right this second, to exist outside of my mind? I ask this because I am continually seeing how stupid I am, getting entangled in all the nonsense of the mind.

Sadhguru: Now, I want you to understand that the mind has many layers and layers of cleverness. Please see within you right now, one part of your mind thinks it's so very clever that it's admitting that it's stupid. If you are really stupid, you wouldn't even know that you are stupid. So the mind goes on playing tricks like this. 'Oh, I know I am stupid; I have declared it to everybody.' That's very smart, you know?

So existing out of your mind — don't get into all these kinds of things. Why do you want to exist out of your mind? Because somebody has told you Buddha was outside his mind. As far as you are concerned, there is no such thing right now. Your purpose is just to understand that your mind functions with whatever limited perception it has had till now; and that's very limited. And with this limitedness, you cannot aspire for something which is beyond or unlimited. If you understand that much, then you will not give too much importance to what your mind is saying. If you try to suppress it, if you try to avoid it, if you try to get out of it, I am telling you, it will be a lifetime of endless deception, because such things cannot happen.

If you just understand the limitations of the mind and accept it for its limitations; if you value the opinions of your mind within those limited spaces that it understands; if the rest of the time, you see that it has no perception of the other aspects of life; and if you just keep yourself open — then what needs to happen, will happen. But if you go on aspiring to somehow kill the mind or to avoid the mind, it will be a futile effort. And in fact, there is really no effort. It is just that you are only trying to enhance the mind.

Nobody aspires to be stupid. Nobody can. If they claim so, they are trying to be over-smart. Everybody would like to at least have a semblance of smartness around them. People act stupid intentionally because that 's their idea of smartness. As long as you function through your mind, you : aspiration is always to be smart. Don't try to go against it; it won't help. It is just that your smartness will take devious ways. Just be straight about it. Yes, you want to be smart; you don't want to be stupid. But at the same time, see the limitations within which the mind is functioning.

See, our driver, Gopal, is a good man, a very balanced good driver. He may be not a Formula One man, but he is a good driver to travel with. If you travel with certain drivers on these roads, you would see, many times, panic breaking out because you overshot a certain point, or your driver got excited because somebody overtook him. But you never saw Gopal doing this in all these days. He is a balanced man and is a good driver. Now can you keep him as your consultant for your spiritual growth also? That's stupid, isn't it?

Similarly, your mind may be good at certain things; use it for that. If you try to consult it for everything, then it will be no good. So just recognize the limitations of your mind.

What's beyond it, don't ask it. What's within its realm, use it.

'These are the two ways — either include everything or exclude everything. Either become infinite, or become zero.'

Seeker: Throughout my life I've always held beauty in high reverence, whether it's looking for the most beautiful things or looking for the beauty in the simple things. Is that simply a significance that *I'm* assigning to beauty? Is it just entertainment? Or is there any spiritual importance to experiencing something as beautiful?

Sadhguru: It is a good way of entertaining yourself. Now, once you label something as 'beautiful', invariably you have to label something else as 'ugly', isn't it? If there's no perspective, there's no beauty, isn't it? You just being overwhelmed with life is different. You labeling something as beautiful and something as ugly is different. The moment I label something as beautiful, naturally I am drawn towards it. I have pleasant thoughts about it, pleasant emotions about it. The moment I label something as ugly, naturally I am repelled from it. Naturally, I have unpleasant thoughts and unpleasant emotions about it. You can't stop it.

You know people are going about telling you, you will love even that which is bad. It's a big lie. Once you have labeled something as bad, it means you don't want to have anything to do with it. Only when you think, 'this is good', you are drawn towards it. Similarly, beauty and ugliness is just good and bad, in one way. It's a visual perception of good and bad, isn't it? So when we live in the world, when we operate as people, maybe we have to identify something about likes and dislikes. You know, if we play with it, it's okay. But that should not rule the fundamentals of who you are within you.

When we utter the word 'spirituality,' what we are saying is, 'I want to become all-inclusive. Or all-exclusive. I want to include everything as a part of myself, or I want to just exclude everything, including myself.' These are the two ways — either include everything or exclude everything. Either become infinite, or become zero. These are the only two ways. There are only two doors to this. If you climb — one, two, three, four, five — there are no doors; it's a trap. There are only two doors. One is the infinite, the other is zero.

So you should either become all-inclusive or you see everything as nothing. These are the two fundamental paths that you will see in this part of the world. There are certain schools of yoga that revere everything, that recognize God in every stone, every tree, everything. That's why you see people worshipping little stones anywhere and everywhere here, because they have been taught God is everywhere. Whether it's a dog, or a cow, or a snake, or whatever, you worship everything because you recognize everything as divine. There is nothing which is other than the divine. There is no Devil in the Eastern way of life. Everything is divine.

And there are other schools of yoga which see everything as absolutely filthy. So if you meet those people, they are always highly abusive people. They abuse everything. For this set of people who see everything as divine, every day their morning and evening is worship. But for that class of yogis, their morning and evening is about abusing God and creation and everything. Every day in the morning they have the choicest of vulgarities to be uttered towards Shiva. Every morning they will start abusing Shiva, his mother, and everything, because they see the Creator and creation as absolutely filthy. Seeing it as filthy is a much quicker way, but it's a very demanding way. You cannot live in social situations. These people cannot be with anybody. They are always alone, because they see the next person as filthy and themselves as filthy too. So they cannot be with anybody. It's a very quick path, but a very rigorous path.

So the other option is to see everything as divine. It makes you pleasant, makes you fit into social situations, makes you go well with people when you recognize the Divine in everybody. This is the other path.

The moment you say something is good and something is bad, you are divided. Something is beautiful, something is ugly; something is divine, something is the Devil – once you divide, there is no end; it's an endless trap. It's simply an endless trap. Just look at it. You have divided the world and you are trying to be all-inclusive. It is just a self-defeating process.

People still retain a strong sense of like and dislike, and they are pursuing spiritual paths. That is the main reason why they find spirituality seems to be so hard. It is not hard. You have created a strong sense of like and dislike. Like and dislike has come because you have identified something as good, something as bad. Once you identify something as bad, including it doesn't arise. It won't happen; it doesn't matter how hard you try. You may pretend; you may speak kindly even to that which you consider bad, but the moment you labeled it as bad, inclusion is not possible. So the spiritual path has become a struggle only because of this.

'If there is any genuine work on this planet, it's only with human beings. With the rest of life you really have no work to do — everything is fine.'

Seeker: It's very inspiring to hear things like 'art for art's sake', 'beauty for beauty's sake', or 'love for love's sake.' How is it possible to live life without getting possessive and attached?

Sadhguru: What has this 'art for art's sake, beauty for beauty's sake, love for love's sake' got to do with possessiveness? This 'art for art's sake' is the artists' way of enshrining their work. See, the laborer on the street works just for food. If you tell him, 'work for work's sake, and don't bother about money and food' (*Laughs*), he'll say, 'No way.' He'll laugh at you. An artist may not be looking for food and money in what he does, but he is seeking pleasure in his activity, isn't it? That's his way of being happy. So art is being done because that's his happiness, because that's the only pleasure he knows in his life. If you stop him from doing that, he will go crazy. If you want to punish an artist, don't put him in a prison. Just take away his tools and tell him he should never do it. He will die.

So it's not art for art's sake. It's art for life's sake, isn't it? So the same goes for everything. People are somehow averse to seeing life as it is. They want to paint life a little more colorfully than the way it is, simply because very few beings have ever tasted life really the way it is. Simple basic life is not sufficient; you have to glorify it in so many ways. It's unfortunate. When you try to glorify life, what it means is, you are making a clear statement: the Creator is an idiot; his job is not good enough; you have to do something else to make it beautiful. But that's not the reality. Creation is so fantastic. If you are willing to merge with it for a moment, you will see there is really no need to do anything. If you just sit here, it's perfect.

If at all you have any work, it's only with the human beings. (*Laughs*) With the rest of the world, you really have no work, isn't it? If at all you have any work, if there is something that needs to be done, it's only the human beings who are broken beings. Everything else is perfect, total, in the way it is, isn't it? The broken human being, we have to patch him up, or we have to demolish him completely and make him see there is something else beyond this. The rest of the work you do is because you cannot sit quietly. The only reason why people are doing everything they're doing is because they cannot sit quietly. That's all it is. Please look at it carefully. If there is any genuine work on this planet, it's only with human beings. With the rest of life you really have no work to do — everything is fine.

These two things are not really connected, but you brought in this question of possessiveness. Why do you want to possess somebody or something? Because that's the only way you know how to include somebody as a part of yourself. Your possessiveness also is yoga. Yoga means to become all-inclusive. Your possessiveness also is yoga, but it's a very stupid yoga, because it's painful yoga. And it will always remain an incomplete yoga, a frustrating yoga, because you are never going to possess everything. You may possess this much, that much, but after that it's frustrating, because so much else remains out of your possession, and it will always be so. It's a dumb yoga, because it will never reach its goal.

So you learn to include everything as a part of yourself, without the need to possess it. See, to enjoy the Himalayas, do I have to write it on a paper and give it to you that these Himalayas belong to you, and it's only your Himalayas? It's stupid, isn't it? But that's what you're asking in life. To enjoy anything, it must be yours, isn't it? Even to enjoy a child, it has to be yours. Somebody has to check your DNA and say it has come from your body only, not from somebody else's body. You cannot enjoy anything the way it is. The only little pleasure that you have in your life is that something belongs to you. And even what belongs to you, if it belongs to everybody, you cannot enjoy it. This is a perversion; this is a disease, isn't it? It must belong to you, and only to you – only then you can enjoy it.

Or your enjoyment is that nobody else has what you have. That is definitely a sickness, isn't it? Your only joy in the world is that you have something that nobody else has – isn't it a sickness? Unfortunately ninety-five per cent of the population is psychologically ill because that's the only pleasure they have. If they wear these clothes, nobody else should be wearing them. If everybody is wearing this, they cannot enjoy it. If they build a house, nobody else should have that kind of house – only then they can enjoy it. This is not joy; this is just illness. You need treatment. Unfortunately, ninety-five per cent of the world needs treatment. It's sad, but that's how it is. Let's enjoy the madhouse. What else to do? That's all the choice we are given. We have to live with crazy people – mentally ill people.

People ask me, 'Why are you going around like a madman when you have no need for anything? Why are you going around trying to do all this?' Because I want to live. I am fed up living with idiots. I would like to see at least a few lively human beings around me (*Laughs*), who are capable of life just for the sake of life. Just being alive is sufficient; they don't have to do anything. I would like to live with such people.

As I said before, one reason why I come to the Himalayas is, it's the only place where, if I walk, there are people who just look at me and recognize who I am. It doesn't matter what I am wearing. Immediately they recognize me, and you see that dignified nod from them. That's all. Nowhere else in the world do I meet such people. It's very rare. This is the only place where I meet dozens of such people. It's like coming home.

'The flower has no use..., but it is the most beautiful dimension of the life-process of a plant. It is the peak of its life.'

Seeker: What is the significance of flowers in worship, if it's not for their beauty?

Sadhguru: Flowers are significant, worship or no worship. If you look at it biologically, flowers are just tools for the plant to reproduce. You may be thinking wonderful things about flowers; you may be thinking these flowers are wonderful ornaments for your gods. But as far as the flower is concerned, it is just trying to attract the bee and reproduce itself. That is all it is doing. In fact, if you look at the whole world biologically, it is just simple, plain reproduction and survival. So that is one way to look at it. Another way is, a flower is the height of life's expression in a plant.

A flower can be many things for people. For somebody, a flower may be God's own face. For the scientist, it is just a stupid attempt at reproduction. But for a mystic, it is the divine blooming in its highest way. Why are flowers used for worship? Why not stones? Why not pebbles? Why not leaves? Why not something else? Look at a person; see the way he inclines himself toward something. If somebody is always thinking of multiplying things, his interest would be in seeds. If somebody is always thinking of shelter and security, his interest will be in the trunk and branches of the tree. If somebody is thinking of pleasure, his interest will be only in fruit. There are people who plant a mango sapling today and sit thinking, 'When it comes how sweet it will be.' They are not interested in the root of the plant, the plant, the leaves, or anything. They don't care what the hell is happening with the plant. They just wait for the fruit. They will never enjoy the process of the plant-growing; every leaf coming out is not a joy for them. For them only fruit matters, and if their neighbor's children don't rob it, only then they will be happy. If their neighbor's children take it away, five years of expectation are gone.

If you look at the plant, flower, fruit and seed, the flower is the most fragile, the most momentary. It is not the same in the evening as you see it in the morning. If you want to enjoy a particular flower, you have to get up early in the morning and see it. If you get up at 10 o'clock in the morning, it won't be the same. It is so fragile. Always the spiritual process has been referred to as a flowering. We don't say 'fruiting' of consciousness. We say 'flowering' of consciousness. Fruit is always talked about in terms of result, in terms of 'something must happen'. You know, you must get something out of it. That aspect is very dominant in the fruit. There is a deep pleasure-seeking in the fruit. But somebody who just enjoys life, he enjoys flowers. It is just a simple and a glorious expression of life. But it has no real purpose; it is not useful for anything.

When I said, let us all plant flowering trees, some of our very practical brahmacharis asked, 'What is the use? Let us plant vendakkai (okra), let us plant pavarakkai (bitter gourd). Why flowering trees?' They're right in many ways. I'm not against them, but I would like to live among flowers and be hungry, rather than live among vendakkais with a full stomach. The flower has no use if you look at it that way, but it is the most beautiful dimension of the life-process of a plant. It is the peak of its life. So when you offer something to that which you consider divine, you want to offer that which is at the peak. You would like to pull out your heart and put it there, but you don't want to put your toe there. Yes? Because whatever is the peak in you, whatever is the highest dimension in you, that you want to give. In a plant, the highest dimension of its life is the flower. So that's what you offer. Not the root, not the stem, not the branches, but the flower.

So, in your life, the greatest thing that you can do to yourself is not to become like a trunk, a root, a seed, but to become like a flower, because a flower is the most useless, but the most accessible. If you are passing this way, even if you are not willing, its fragrance enters your nostrils. You have no choice about it, isn't it? Even if you're insensitive, still you feel something happening. All the other aspects don't have that. So the whole effort of any spiritual process is to become like a flower. The flower has become symbolic. The flower has become synonymous with offering.

'A blessing is gasoline. It's a piece of energy. It's not good wishes.'

Seeker: Sadhguru, I've seen you blessing people's rudraksha beads. What is a blessing exactly?

Sadhguru: See, me or anybody saying, 'all the best to you', is not a blessing; it is just a wish. A wish is just a hope. It is not substantiated by anything. It is just a nice thought.

A blessing is not a thought. A blessing is not an emotion. A blessing is a piece of energy. If you've made yourself fluid enough (so that you are not a burnt pot), if you're just loose energy, then you can take a little bit of that and give. If you are a properly burnt pot, you can't take anything out of it because it's crystallized. So, a blessing is not a good thing; nor is it a bad thing. It's just something that hastens you. It's like gas. (*Laughter*) Gas in the car. (*Laughter*) Oh, not you. I meant gasoline (*More laughter*). You put gasoline into the tank, you can move. If you are pushing your car and going, you know how far your home is? A long, long way, isn't it? You've got gas in the tank; you are there in no time, isn't it? Whatever the distance, it's no big deal. So a blessing is like gas in the tank. It's not a wish; it's not a thought; it's not an emotion. It's not good, it's not bad. It's just gasoline.

That's if you want a moving car. But you may be somebody who enjoys a parked car. A moving car is dangerous; it could crash, isn't it? A parked car is definitely far safer. Yes? A lot of people have chosen to live in a parked car. Morning, of course, becomes afternoon; and afternoon, of course, becomes evening; and evening, of course, becomes night. Fall becomes winter; winter becomes spring; spring becomes summer; and then autumn again. It looks like you are going somewhere; there's so much change of scenery. It's exciting enough. But if you are a little loony that to go a certain distance you are willing to risk your life, then you drive a car. You want a moving car, isn't it? A parked car is a damn safe car. It's good; you could very well live there; no problem. It's just that you don't go anywhere, that's all. But now you want to go somewhere. There are drunken drivers on the street (*Laughs*), but still you want to go somewhere. Now you need gas.

So, a blessing is gasoline. It's a piece of energy. It's not good wishes. Unfortunately, most people refuse it when it comes to them because they don't realize it's a blessing. They expect that a blessing means it will always come in a particular way. No. Especially when it comes from me, it comes in so many ways that you've not imagined. And you know how I am. (*Laughs*) It's always packaged in ways that you don't usually expect.

Last winter this happened. A tiny little Michigan bird just enjoyed the fall time a little too much and didn't start its journey south early enough. It started a little late in the winter and tried to fly out, and it just froze and fell down. A cow was passing this way and it dropped a heap of dung, and the dung fell right over the bird. But the warmth of the dung slowly defrosted the bird, and he started feeling good and started tweeting happily because he had recovered from a frozen state. A cat was going this way. It heard the tweet, looked around; then he saw the tweet was coming from inside the dung. So he pulled the bird out of the dung and ate him up.

So what you need to understand is, whoever heaps you up in shit need not necessarily be your enemy. Whoever pulls you out of shit need not necessarily be your friend. (*Laughter*) And above all, when you are in a heap of shit, learn to keep your mouth shut. (*Laughter*)

So how it comes, you don't know. That's why you must keep all the windows and doors open. You never know how it comes. It gets packaged in so many different ways. If it's packaged in obvious ways, it'll go waste. So it's always packaged in most unusual ways. It's a question of creativity (*Laughs*), how deceptively you package it. The more deceptive it is, the better it is. If it's a very obvious way, okay, but it doesn't do the same thing as when a blessing enters you without you thinking it's a blessing. So it's always packaged in so many different ways. I have been quite creative. (*Laughter*)

'You can't teach madness to people. They have to be infected.'

Seeker: Sadhguru, you once said, 'Transmission is more important than teaching. Teaching is only a way of knocking on the door.' Could you explain what you meant by that?

Sadhguru: (*Somebody's cell phone rings*) See, teaching is like that. (*Laughter*) It is just a noise that I make so that you take the call. (*Laughter*) Things don't happen because of the great quality of music that's coming out of the cell phone. The music is to remind you that you must take the call.

So teaching is just to remind you that you must take the call. The noises are being made to remind you that you must take the call, because truth cannot be taught. If somebody believes that he is teaching the truth, that's one big lie. How can you do it? Because when we say 'truth', we are talking about that which is the basis of everything, that which contains everything. What is partial is a lie. Only that which is total, only that which is absolute can be true. The rest is a lie. It may be a different state of reality but it's a lie.

When you sleep and you dream, the dream state can be so powerful that in your experience it can seem real. But the moment you wake up, you say, 'I had a dream.' You are admitting that that was not the truth. Even though the experience was so powerful, still you call it a dream. So we call something 'truth' only if it is complete. In any way if it is partial, we say this is not it. So that which is absolute, how can it be taught?

You can speak and teach only through language. Not necessarily through spoken language; maybe sign language, but still language. The basis of language itself is the duality between sound and silence. So right now there are any number of people here who do not understand the English language. But the best part is they are sitting as alert and as still as the people who understand English, because they know better. They know that what Sadhguru has to offer is not in his words. (*Applause*) Those who clap are not those people. (*Laughter*) They understand the language! (*Laughter*)

So when we say 'truth', we are not talking about an ideology; we are not talking about a philosophy; we are not talking about a scripture. We are talking about that which is the basis of our existence. We are talking about that which is the source of who we are right now. Even if you have a powerful emotion within you, you become speechless. Language seems insufficient. If you have a tender feeling towards somebody, suddenly language becomes insufficient. You would like to touch them and somehow convey to them; you believe that they will understand. They don't but you believe they do. (*Laughter*) They don't, you know. Don't have such hopes. People don't. (*Laughs*)

So how to transmit that which is the basis of your existence? How to teach the basis of your existence? It can be transmitted. Any number of times I have been saying this (I am trying to change my terminology now for sexist reasons): 'I am laying eggs all over the place. Some day they will hatch somewhere. Lots of them all over the place. When the situation becomes right, they will hatch.' Recently, somebody reminded me that this egg business is a very female thing. So I said, 'Okay, from now on I will say I am releasing lot of spores. When the right kind of situation happens, they will sprout.' (*Laughs*) Just a small sexist change (*Laughs*), but it means the same thing. (*Laughs*)

Do we have that poem what I sent as a message for today? Yesterday they asked me for a message for Guru Poornima. So I just wrote one more bad poem. With great care I have remained uneducated, so I can only write bad poems. (*Laughs*) It takes much more effort to remain uneducated in this world than to become educated. Do you know this? Because to live in this world, to function in this world and still not to learn anything from anybody around you, is not a small feat. To remain uncivilized, uncultured, uninfluenced by anything around you, is a much bigger feat than getting educated, cultured and civilized. Generally, people who manage that could never be active and effective in the world that they live in. That's why most of the mystics withdrew, because if you become cultured or civilized, you cannot be a mystic. Civilization means the circumstances in which you are living has deeply influenced you and molded you in a certain way. So, refusing to be influenced, refusing to be molded by situations around you, perceiving everything directly, not allowing your scriptures, your culture, your teachers, your parents and everybody else to civilize you, takes a lot of conscious effort. So because of that I write bad poetry. Please bear with me.

This is titled 'Guru Pournami':

In search of Truth
I did the sublime and the weird

The blessed Guru arrived
Had my knowledge routed

With his staff touched the spot sacred
Left me with this Madness infected

This Madness without cure
But is liberation for sure

When I saw even horrific disease
Can transmit with ease

I took the liberty
Of maddening Humanity.

You can't teach madness to people. They have to be infected.

Infection is always a transmission, isn't it? *(Laughs)* It's not easy to get it. *(Laughs)* When you were in school, you would have tried. When you don't want to go to school, you want to catch diphtheria for a day. But it doesn't come, you know. Have you tried? You want at least to catch the 'flu. The damn thing doesn't come. *(Laughs)* It's not easy.

You have to be ripe and the right kind of things have to come your way; only then it happens. Even a disease, when you want it, you won't get it. *(Laughs)* So this is also just like that. Because you want it, you don't get it. You have to make yourself vulnerable, receptive. The spores are all over the place. If you are vulnerable, you will get it. It will catch you. Those who are vulnerable will anyway catch it. It doesn't matter whether they came to the program or not. The program is just about making you vulnerable. The teaching is just about making you vulnerable. But it is not the real thing. That is why we can train teachers to do it, because their work is just to make somebody vulnerable. They themselves are not doing anything.

I am sure for many teachers this is their experience: in the seven-day programs that they conduct, the new participants are going through experiences that the teachers themselves have never known. It is happening to other people, but obviously not because of them. But they are very important, because they are like the cell phone ringing; they are like the door knocking.

If it doesn't ring, who will take the call? Your phone is on silent; I am calling you and calling you and calling you; but they're all 'missed calls'. (*Laughter*) It takes somebody to make some noise; otherwise life will remain a missed call. So teachers are very important. Without the noise of teaching, there will be no transmission. Actually, it would be wrong to say 'no transmission'; there will be some transmission, but it will become very minimal. Only with the teaching the vulnerability has increased, and because of that, more spores are being made use of.

I want you to understand this simple thing has happened to you even physically. One little cell existed; one little sperm found itself in the right place. And see how much life has happened? If it had not gotten into the right womb, if it had fallen somewhere else, this wouldn't have happened. A very sophisticated mechanism has happened, isn't it, out of that one little sperm? It is just that it has to enter the right place. Then it happens. Otherwise it won't. This is just like that. It's on a different sphere, on a different dimension, but still the same. Nobody can talk you into pregnancy. Fortunately (*Laughter*), such a thing has never happened.

'Allow the mountains to happen to you.'

Seeker: Traveling around these mountains, I forget myself, my family and everything. Why is this, Sadhguru?

Sadhguru: (*Laughs*) We should ask your family. You heard

the question? When he's traveling around Himalayas, he forgets himself, his family and everything, whatever that 'everything' is.

All the petty things that you knew in your life, you forgot. You must, because the mountains are so overwhelming. The very reason why you come to the Himalayas is to be overwhelmed by the Himalayas. Not to see and comment, 'Okay, this is beautiful, that is beautiful.' Not for that. To simply look at them, be overwhelmed, burst into tears, go crazy with the mountains. That's why you come here; not to say pretty things about the mountains and go. If you are looking at them and saying, 'Oh, beautiful,' you have not seen anything.

It happened like this. Lao Tzu used to go for a walk in the evenings. One day Lao Tzu's close friend came and said, 'A great professor has come from somewhere. He wishes to walk with you.'

Lao Tzu said, 'The condition is, he must not speak. When I am walking, no talking. Only if he is willing, let him come. Otherwise I don't want him to walk with me.'

Then this friend went and told the professor, 'You should not speak when he is walking; you must walk silently with him.' He said fine, and both of them came to Lao Tzu.

They started walking together and found themselves walking

towards a glorious sunset. Then the professor looked at it and looked at Lao Tzu. Lao Tzu was walking, absolutely expressionless. The professor looked around, wanting to say something to somebody. Then he said, 'Isn't it beautiful?' In those days, they didn't know 'Wow'. (*Laughter*) It's a recent expression.

Lao Tzu just turned around and left. The friend got scared and ran after Lao Tzu. 'What happened? What happened?'

'Your friend talks too much!' said Lao Tzu.

The friend said, 'What is this? He just said the sunset is beautiful.'

Lao Tzu said, 'No, he speaks too much. He speaks too much about things that he doesn't know, that he doesn't experience, that he's not touched by. He's not overwhelmed by what's happening. He's just talking. I don't want to walk with him.' He just walked away.

So you come to Himalayas not to say, 'Oh, its beautiful' and 'Wow'. You must burst and go crazy with the mountains, because they are overwhelming. They are not there to receive pretty words from you. If you just look at them, you must just crack open. Your family should evaporate. Everything should evaporate. You must simply crack open.

It's too big. It's too enormous. Not just in size — in ways that you will not understand right now. Allow the mountains to happen to you.

Isha Foundation

Isha Foundation is a non-religious, not-for-profit, public service organization that addresses all aspects of human well-being. From its powerful yoga programs for inner transformation to its inspiring social and environmental projects, Isha activities are designed to create an inclusive culture as a basis for global peace and development.

This integral approach has gained worldwide recognition, reflected in Isha Foundation's Special Consultative Status with the Economic and Social Council (ECOSOC) of the United Nations. Hundreds of thousands of volunteers support the Foundation's work in over 200 centers across the globe.

Sadhguru

A profound mystic and visionary humanitarian, Sadhguru is a spiritual Master with a difference. An arresting blend of profundity and pragmatism, his life and work serve as a reminder that inner sciences are not an esoteric discipline from an outdated past, but vitally relevant to our times.

With speaking engagements that take him around the world,

Sadhguru is widely sought after by prestigious global forums such as the United Nations Millennium Peace Summit, the Australian Leadership Retreat and the World Economic Forum.

Isha Yoga Programs

Isha Yoga offers a unique possibility for individuals to empower themselves and reach their full potential. Designed by Sadhguru to suit individuals from every social and cultural background, Isha Yoga programs extend a rare opportunity for self-discovery and inner transformation under the guidance of an enlightened Master.

Isha Yoga Center

Isha Yoga Center, founded under the aegis of Isha Foundation, is located at the Velliangiri Foothills amidst a forest reserve with abundant wildlife. Created as a powerful center for inner growth, this popular destination attracts people from all parts of the world.

Dhyanalinga Yogic Temple

The Dhyanalinga is a powerful and unique energy form, the essence of yogic sciences. The Dhyanalinga Yogic Temple is a meditative space that does not ascribe to any particular faith or belief system nor require any ritual, prayer or worship. The vibrational energies of the Dhyanalinga allow even those unaware of meditation to experience a deep state of meditativeness, revealing the essential nature of life.

Isha Rejuvenation

Isha Rejuvenation offers unique, carefully scientifically structured programs designed by Sadhguru to bring vibrancy and optimal balance to one's life energies, thus facilitating healthy living as well as the prevention and uprooting of chronic ailments.

Action for Rural Rejuvenation

Action for Rural Rejuvenation (ARR) is a holistic social outreach program whose primary objective is to improve the overall health and quality of life of the rural poor.

Dedicated teams of qualified and trained personnel operate ARR's Mobile Health Clinics, which currently provide free basic health care to more than 4,000 villages in South India.

Project GreenHands

Project GreenHands (PGH) is an ecological initiative of Isha Foundation to prevent and reverse environmental degradation and enable sustainable living. The project aims to create 10% additional green cover in Tamil Nadu. Drawing on the participation of a wide cross-section of people, 114 million trees will be planted by the year 2010.

Isha Vidhya — An Isha Education Initiative

Isha Vidhya provides affordable, high quality primary school education to villages across South India's Tamil Nadu state.

Over the coming years, Isha Vidhya will set up 206 schools designed specifically to create confident, English-speaking, computer literate children. Students will graduate prepared to pursue higher education.

Isha Home School

Isha Home School, set in the tranquil surroundings of the Velliangiri Foothills, offers a stimulating environment for the inner blossoming of each child. Isha Home School helps each student reach his or her true potential and enhances his or her natural and latent talents while maintaining high standards of academic excellence.

Isha Business

Isha Business is a venture spearheaded and promoted by Isha Foundation to bring a touch of Isha into people's lives through numerous products and services, such as architectural and interior design, construction, furniture, crafts, clothing and much more. The proceeds benefit the poorest of the poor through Action for Rural Rejuvenation.

Contact Us:

INDIA

Isha Yoga Center
Velliangiri Foothills
Semmedu (P.O.)
Coimbatore-641 114, India
Tel. +91-422-2515345
info@ishafoundation.org

USA

Isha Foundation Inc./Isha Institute of Inner Sciences
951, Isha Lane
McMinnville, TN-37110, USA
Tel: +1-866-424-ISHA (4742)
usa@ishafoundation.org

UNITED KINGDOM

Isha Institute of Inner Sciences
PO Box 559,
Isleworth, TW7 5WR, UK
Tel: +44-7956998729
uk@ishafoundation.org

For more information and your local center please visit our website:

www.ishafoundation.org

Dhyanalinga – The Silent Revolution

This richly illustrated book presents a deeper definition of yoga and its metaphysical essence. It culminates in the presentation of the Dhyanalinga.

Encounter the Enlightened – Conversations with the Master

This book captures interactive moments with the Master. It is an invitation to the reader to go beyond words and experience the wisdom of the boundless.

Eternal Echoes – The Sacred sounds through the Mystic

A compelling and provocative collection of poetry by Sadhguru. This book of high artistic merit moves us into the timeless, eternal reality of an enlightened being.

Flowers on the Path

A compilation of articles created by Sadhguru for the Speaking Tree column of the Times of India. These articles bring infusions of beauty, humor, clarity and insight into our lives.

Midnights with the Mystic – A Little Guide to Freedom and Bliss

Presented in a series of conversations between seeker, the co-author Cheryl Simone, and enlightened Master, Sadhguru, this captivating book challenges us to embrace the possibility of a higher reality, a peak of consciousness. Available at bookstores and online booksellers such as amazon.com and Barnes & Noble.

Find further inspiration in Sadhguru's profound insights on a variety of life-relevant topics, combined in pairs of two to the following revealing books:

- Enlightenment: What It Is & Leave Death Alone

- Dissolving Your Personality & Good and Bad Divides the World

- Ancient Technology for the Modern Mind & Culture of Peace

- Dimension Beyond the Physical & Circus of the Intellect

- Living Life to the Fullest & Unleashing the Mind

- Is Spirituality a Science & Isha: Sacred Space for Self Transformation